Climbing the
Ladder of Success
in Highheels
Backgrounds of Professional Women

Research in Clinical Psychology, No. 9

Peter E. Nathan, Series Editor

Professor and Chairman
Department of Clinical Psychology
Rutgers, the State University of New Jersey

Other Titles in This Series

Climbing the Ladder of Success in Highheels

Backgrounds of Professional Women

by
Jill A. Steinberg

UMI RESEARCH PRESS
Ann Arbor, Michigan

Produced and distributed by
UMI Research Press
an imprint of
University Microfilms International
Ann Arbor, Michigan 48106

Library of Congress Cataloging in Publication Data

Steinberg, Jill A. (Jill Ann)
 Climbing the ladder of success in highheels.

 (Research in clinical psychology ; no. 9)
 Revision of author's thesis (Ph.D.)–Ohio State
University, 1978.
  Bibliography: p.
  Includes index.
  1. Women in the professions–United States.
2. Women–Employment–Social aspects–United States.
I. Title. II. Series.

HQ1426.S825 1984   305.5'53'088042   83-15921
ISBN 0-8357-1491-8

This book is dedicated to Ethel Steinberg, my mother and best friend, a woman who has been an incredible role model of a nontraditional professional and mother.

Contents

Acknowledgments

I feel truly fortunate to acknowledge (for the first time publicly) the following list of people—all individuals without whom this book would not have been completed.

Much thanks and appreciation to Ethel Steinberg, my mother, for the honesty, trust, confidence and love I have always known was there for me in my struggle to become an independent woman. In addition, thanks for our Jewish heritage which has always encouraged furthering one's education.

To you, Jaques Kaswan, my adviser and strongest source of academic encouragement, I give thanks for your constructive criticism, perceptive insights and sense of humor. Most of all, I thank you for the support that enabled me to regain my academic confidence and complete the clinical psychology doctoral program.

To you, Anne Berry, I give thanks for helping me become a loving and strong Professional Woman—for your modeling and encouragement which has enabled me to learn to work and play—to complete a book, earn tenure and even run a marathon when it is not ski season.

Eric Hoffman—without your close and loyal friendship I would not have completed this book. Thanks go to you for your patience, concern and undying support.

Keith Widaman, my statistical consultant, much thanks to you for your help analyzing my data. No doubt without your thorough knowledge of statistical analysis, your ability to clearly articulate that information to me and your consistently supportive manner, I would still be at the computer center.

To the rest of the doctoral committee—I give sincere thanks to Sandy Mamrak for the helpful advice you have shared with me and the role model you have been throughout my years at Ohio State. I would like to thank Nancy Betz for the time and useful feedback you gave to me during this project.

I would also like to acknowledge and thank the women whose participation helped to make this study possible and the women at the Office of Women's Studies at Ohio State University for the small grant which helped finance the project.

List of Tables

List of Figures

1

Introduction

Fundamental assumptions about the two sexes are being questioned by educators, scientists and feminists (Orlofsky & Stake, 1981; Adams, Lawrence & Cook, 1979; Maccoby, 1975). In particular, these people have been interested in women's social, educational and occupational positions. Support for a reassessment of women's roles has come largely from the women's movement, a movement which attempts to expose the discrimination women feel in their social roles, play, education and work.

Concurrent with this growing pressure for awareness of "women's place" in American society has been an increase in research literature on women and work. This information covers educational pursuits and trends in women's work (Randour, Strasburg & Lipmen-Blumen, 1982; Best, 1981; Knepper, Elliott & Albright, 1981; Ahern & Scott, 1981; Saslaw, 1981; Scopino, 1980; Spence, 1978-79; Lloyd, 1975; Daniels, 1975), determinants of career choice (Needels-Richardson, 1983; Komarovsky, 1982; Kaplan, 1981; Lemkau, 1979; Ruddick & Daniels, 1977; Zuckerman, 1981, 1978, 1976; Bachtold, 1976; Baruch, 1976; Osipow, 1975; Birnbaum, 1975; Kundsin, 1974; Zytowski, 1969; Astin, 1969), the dual role of worker and mother (Gray, 1983; Sckaran, 1982; VanMeter & Agronow, 1982; Houseknecht & Macke, 1981; Kelly, 1982; Yogev, 1981; Beckman & Houser, 1979; Hoffman, 1974a; Bryson, Bryson, Licht & Licht, 1976), and discriminatory practices against women (Martin, 1982; Hall & Sandler, 1982; Robinowitz, Nadelson & Notman, 1981; Wallis, Gilder & Thaler, 1981; Levitin, Quinn, & Staines, 1973; Sutter & Miller, 1973; Goldberg, 1968; Astin & Bayer, 1972).

The discussions of women's career goals have had two main foci: 1) the conditions in American society which function to keep women in mainly nonprofessional status (Super, 1980; Safilios-Rothschild, 1979; Brown, 1979; Steinberg, 1976; Theodore, 1971; Bernard, 1973, 1971, 1964; White, 1970; Epstein, 1971a, 1971b, 1971c; Rossi, 1965a, 1965c); and 2) the variables related to women's professional career choices (Lyson & Brown, 1982; Greenglass & Devins, 1982; Betz & Hackett, 1981; Illfelder, 1980; Bachtold, 1976; Connolly, Burks & Rogers, 1976; Zuckerman, 1981, 1978, 1976; Osipow, 1975; Hoffman,

1972, 1974b; Mednick, Tangri, & Hoffman, 1976; Rand, 1971; Hoyt & Kennedy, 1958).

The research exploring conditions associated with career-orientation divides women into three main categories: 1) women who are primarily concerned with pursuing the traditional homemaking role (labeled homemaking-oriented or full-time homemakers in the literature); 2) women who are aspiring to careers in traditional female occupations (labeled Traditional career-oriented women); and 3) women who are oriented towards a nontraditional male-dominated occupation (labeled Role Innovators or Pioneer career women or Nontraditional career-oriented women). The literature defines traditional careers as those in which at least two-thirds of the individuals employed are women (e.g., teaching, nursing) and pioneer careers as those in which at least two-thirds of the individuals employed are males (e.g., medicine, law).

This division of labor into women's and men's fields remained relatively stable between 1900–1960 (Almquist, 1974; Gross, 1971). The last two decades, however, have marked a period of change, with nontraditional career choices and combinations of choices becoming increasingly popular, especially among college women (Farmer, 1983). The proportion of women in the labor force has increased from 37.4% of all women 16 years of age or over employed in 1960, to 50.1% in 1978 (U.S. Dept. of Labor, 1979; Daniels, 1975; Schiffler, 1975). The majority of married women are employed and expect to continue to be employed throughout the 1980s (U.S. Women's Bureau, 1979).

This employment increase coincided with an increase in women oriented towards careers at college entry (Harmon, 1981; Montanelli Jr. & Mamrak, 1976; Carnegie Commission, 1973). From 1974 to 1979, the enrollment of women in higher education increased by 32.5% (Grant & Eiden, 1982) and in 1980, the number of full-time women students exceeded the number of full-time male students (Tapper, 1981). In 1972 there were 74 women per 100 men in college; by 1981 there were 108 women in college to every 100 men. Women also account for a majority of the part-time and two-year college students. The enrollment of women in graduate and professional schools rose about 75% between 1970 and 1975 (Gray, 1983) and women presently comprise 45% of graduate school enrollment. In addition, since 1960, women have assumed more positions in the traditionally male-dominated majors and professions, in some cases doubling and tripling the number or proportion of women in these fields.

Although these changes occurring since the 60's appear to be substantial, the number and proportion of women presently involved in nontraditional fields is still quite small, since the original number of women involved in the professions was so small. For example, what has been stated as a dramatic increase of women in the field of law, really means the proportion of women lawyers and judges more than doubled from 2.8% to 7.0% (Garfinkle, 1975).

Similarly, between 1962 and 1974, the increases for women were from 5.5% to 9.8% of physicians, 10.4% to 16.5% pharmacists, and 19.2% to 30.9% college/university teachers (Garfinkle, 1975). Women gained only 3.5% of top-level administrative positions in higher education institutions between 1975 and 1979; as of 1979, women and minorities combined held less than 25% of the top university administrative positions (Knepper et al, 1981).

Because women's educational level has been found to be consistently correlated with the probability of women being employed outside the home (Schiffler, 1975), educational statistics parallel the employment statistics; i.e., women's educational levels were relatively stable from 1900–1960 and have increased since 1960 (Goldberg & Shiflett, 1981; Ginzberg, 1966). During the 70's, the number of women earning degrees increased at every level (Randour et al, 1982). In the 1940's, the proportion of all bachelor's or first professional degrees earned by women was about 40% and the proportion of all master's degrees granted to women was 15% (Theodore, 1971). By 1979, women comprised 50.1% of first year two-year and four-year college students, 48.2% of students granted bachelor's degrees, 49.1% of the master's recipients, and 28.1% of the doctorates (Randour et al., 1982). In the field of medicine, first year enrollment advanced from 9.1% of total enrollment in 1969–70 to 23.4% in 1975–76. Degrees awarded in medicine went from 8.4% in 1970 to 23.0% in 1979 (Randour et al., 1982). Enrollment in dentistry increased from 1.6% to 17.0% (Chronicle of Higher Education, 1978; Grant & Eiden, 1982). The percentage of women earning law degrees rose from 5% to 28% between 1970 and 1979 (Randour et al., 1982).

Although these statistics demonstrate that women have always received an education and held jobs, and that employment outside of the home is on the increase, there is ample documentation that women rarely obtain high status positions or stay in careers (Randour et al, 1982; Knepper et al, 1981; Epstein, 1971b, 1971c; Theodore, 1971; Mednick, Tangri, & Hoffman, 1976; Daniels, 1975). At the end of the 1970's, married women in high status professions remained an extremely small group, 6/10 of 1% of all employed married women (Benenson, 1981). The literature suggests that those women in American society who do in fact achieve professional success remain the rare exception and are often perceived and labeled as "deviants" (Collier, 1982; Steinberg, 1976; Wolman & Frank, 1975, 1973; Epstein, 1971b; Bernard, 1971).

Looking at American cultural definitions of sex roles makes this "deviancy" phenomenon more understandable. The concept "role" used here refers to "the sum of norms directed towards a person occupying a given position or status" (Holter, 1970, p. 54). The male role is described as "Instrumental"; the female role as "Expressive" (Parsons & Bales, 1955). More specifically, the male instrumental cluster incorporates such behaviors or adjectives as competent, independent, objective, active, competitive, logical, able to make decisions easily, self-confident, dominant and desiring prestigious careers for their own needs. Females, on the other hand, are expected to exhibit the expressive qualities of gentleness, kindness, warmth, sensitivity, emotionality, passivity, dependence, tactfulness, noncompetitiveness and desiring positions where they can help others (Adams, Lawrence & Cook, 1979; Parsons & Bales, 1955; Broverman, Vogel, Broverman, Clarkson, & Rosenkrantz, 1972; Osipow, 1975). Clearly these sets of adjectives which have been stable over time set up expectations which portray males as the competent-doers; females as the emotional-feelers (Broverman et al., 1972).

In essence, then, what this means is that women are not expected to assume professional roles, and by definition those women who do achieve professional status and exhibit instrumental attributes are deviant, since they are perceived as violating the expectations ascribed to them as women (Williams, 1973; Hawkins & Tiedeman, 1975). This deviant notion can be explained by the normative paradigm of social order. This theoretical model assumes behavior of individuals is largely culture specific because behavior is determined mostly by the normative standards and institutionalized expectations within a given society (Frieze, Parsons, Johnson, Ruble & Zellman, 1978; Lemert, 1972). According to this approach, social order exists and is imposed on particular interactions from outside the interaction through socialization processes within the culture (Hawkins & Tiedeman, 1975). Socialization through such established societal institutions as the family, school systems and the professions results in the internalization of rules and consensus about expected behaviors by the majority of the members within the given culture. Thus, the normative view implies a static, consistent and rather deterministic view of behavioral expectations and actual behaviors performed within the given society's social structure. This model relates more to these nontraditional professions which deviate from the expressive role than to those traditional professions which incorporate many aspects of the expressive role.

In spite of the fact that norms against careers for women have persisted, and contradictions exist between what is considered appropriate behavior required for professional success and appropriate behavior for women, there are women who choose the highly valued and economically rewarding male-dominated professions (Lemkau, 1979; Yogev, 1983; Bernard, 1971; Epstein, 1971b; Merton, 1964). Can the channeling of women into nontraditional careers be explained by any particular framework or theory? Several conceptual frameworks address this issue. Personality theorists would emphasize underlying personality characteristics such as autonomy, ambition, creativity, independence or strength, to explain why some women become pioneer career women (Blakeney, Schottstaedt & Sekula, 1982; O'Connell, 1980; Bachtold, 1976; Betz & Hackett, 1981; Tangri, 1972; Rand, 1968; Allport, 1961). Social learning theorists would stress that observational learning from powerful and nurturant role models accounts for the ability of some women to assume high status male-dominated careers (Lunneborg, 1982; Stake, 1981;

Walker, 1981; Basow & Howe, 1980; Kingdon & Sedlacek, 1981; Erkut & Mokros, 1981; Bandura, 1969; Rotter, Chance & Phares, 1973). Feminists, on the other hand, would give credit to the women's movement, with its emphasis on raising women's consciousness to question traditional assumptions and values, for women becoming nontraditionally career oriented (Frieze et al., 1978; Freeman, 1973; 1975; Hole & Levine, 1973). Or, it might be argued that nontraditional women, more than other women, had opportunities such as their higher social class or cultural background, available to them which positively influenced their nontraditional career development. (Almquist & Angrist, 1971). Theoretical frameworks will be examined more fully in the discussion chapter in terms of their ability to explain patterns of individual variables associated with women's nontraditional career development.

In addition to this broad conceptual issue, more specific questions need addressing. For example, why do these women decide to confront the traditional female stereotype and become nontraditional career women? Are these women different from those women who choose more traditionally-oriented female careers or women who become fulltime homemakers? Were there events or people in their lives which positively influenced them to become nontraditional career women? Are nontraditional women as a group similar or are there characteristics only specific to women in a particular profession? Some of these questions have been explored in previous research studies. There seems to be evidence from the literature that the presence of nontraditional career aspirations in women are correlated with several variables. The variables addressed in this paper will be divided into five areas: employment background variables, education variables, family background variables, environmental variables, and self-perception/personal characteristic variables.

Employment Background Variables

Women who have had a large number of jobs and a wide variety of previous experiences are more likely to aspire to pioneer careers (Burlew, 1982; Almquist & Angrist, 1971; Angrist & Almquist, 1975). This research has been interpreted to mean that these women sought out many jobs and experiences in order to realistically examine their nontraditional career goals. In addition, those women who have been involved in a women's support group are more likely to persist with their career goals (Riger, 1974; Kirkpatrick, 1975; Phelps & Astin, 1975; Freeman, 1975).

Education Variables

The literature suggests that pioneer career women are more likely to have received positive support from a significant professor or other influential role model (Daniels, 1975; Carnegie Commission, 1973; Almquist & Angrist, 1971;

Steinberg, 1976; Dunn & Dunn, 1977; Stafford, 1966; Combs & Tolbert, 1980; Heins, Hendricks & Martindale, 1982; Erickson, 1981, Basow & Howe, 1980; Kingdon & Sedlacek, 1981; Lunneborg, 1982).

Family Background Variables

The most consistent findings in the literature on family background variables concern mother's employment status and the woman's birth order. The literature strongly indicates that women with employed mothers are more career-oriented (Lunneborg, 1982; Keith, 1981; Lemkau, 1979; Dellas, 1979; Lozoff, 1974; Helson, 1972; Hoffman, 1972; Almquist & Angrist, 1971; Tangri, 1972; Lovett, 1969; Ginzberg, 1966) than women in general. In addition, a nontraditional professional mother is more likely present in the lives of those women who become pioneer women (Burlew, 1982; Zuckerman, 1981; Lemkau 1979; Tangri, 1972). Father's with nontraditional or traditional careers may have similar effects on their daughters; father's and daughter's careers, however, have not been consistently researched together. There is substantial evidence that first borns have been more likely to choose nontraditional career goals (Needels-Richardson, 1983; Heins, Hendricks & Martindale 1982; Lemkau 1979; Hennig, 1974; Anderson, 1974; Cartwright, 1972; Fakouri, 1974; Gormly, 1968; Rosenberg & Sutton-Smith, 1968; Sutton-Smith & Rosenberg, 1970). There is some research which suggests that the absence of male siblings in associated with women who are more likely to aspire to nontraditional careers (Hennig, 1974; Astin, 1969, 1967).

Other variables which have been less thoroughly investigated include religious background and perceptions of the woman's childhood relationship with her mother. Jewish and Unitarian women have been shown to be the most likely and Catholic women the least likely to pursue pioneer career plans (Karman, 1973). Women developing towards nontraditional careers are more likely to have perceived their childhood relationships with their mothers as hostile (Kundsin, 1974; Hennig, 1974; Hoffman, 1972; Nagley, 1971).

Research discussing socio-economic status (SES) as determined by parents' education or family income, is inconsistent and suggests that SES is not related to women's career choices (Almquist & Angrist, 1971; Siegel & Curtis, 1963). One study, however, comparing doctoral students with women who did not continue their formal education beyond a bachelor's degree suggests that doctoral women were more likely to have more highly educated parents (Astin, 1969). Recent research also supports that nontraditional women are more likely to have highly educated parents (Burlew, 1982; Zuckerman, 1982, 1981; Heins et al., 1982; Lemkau, 1979).

Environmental Variables

Environmental variables which have been previously researched relate to marital status. Results indicate that nontraditional career women more often remain single (Heins et al., 1982; Kaplan, 1982; Benenson, 1981; Almquist & Angrist, 1971; Rossi, 1965a; Astin, 1969) and if they get married, they have fewer children (Astin, 1969; Manis & Hoffman, 1974; Houseknecht & Macke, 1981).

Self-Perception/Personal Characteristics Variables

Self-perception and personal characteristic variables which have been examined along with women's career goals include intelligence, attractiveness, height and strength. There is some research to suggest that nontraditional career women perceive themselves as more intelligent (Stoloff, 1973; Rand, 1968) and more attractive (Birnbaum, 1975; Rand, 1968) than their peers.

Research discussing women's physical height and strength has not been investigated except in a pilot study (Zuckerman, 1976) in spite of findings which show that self-perceived height is related to status for men (Rump & Delin, 1973). The pilot study does suggest that very tall women are more likely to pursue nontraditional career goals; similarly, self-perceived strength also correlates with nontraditional career goals.

Summary of Expectations Found in the Literature

Employment Background Variables

(*E1*)   Nontraditional professional women are more likely to have experienced a large number and wide variety of *previous job experiences.*

(*E2*)   Those women who have experienced a *women's (support) group* will perceive this experience as having positively influenced their career commitment.

Education Variables

(*E3*)   Many of these pioneer women will have received *positive support from a professor or* other influential *role model* during their college and post-college training.

Family Background Variables

(*E4*)   There are significant positive correlations between nontraditional career status and being the *daughter of an employed mother.*

(*E5*)   Daughters' nontraditional career performance will be correlated with *mothers' nontraditional career performance.*

(*E6*)   There are significant positive correlations between nontraditional career status and the status of *first born.*

(*E7*)   There are significant positive correlations between nontraditional career status and the status of *female without male siblings.*

(*E8*)   Career-oriented women are most likely to perceive their *childhood relationship* with their mother as more *hostile* than nurturant.

(*E9*)   Women who are daughters of *Jewish or Unitarian* parents are more likely to be nontraditional in their career goals than daughters of parents with other religious backgrounds.

Environmental Variables

(*E10*)   Nontraditional career women more often remain *single,* or if they get married they have *fewer children.*

Self-Perception/Personal Characteristic Variables

(*E11*)   *Self-perceived intelligence* correlates positively with nontraditional career goals and commitment.

(*E12*)   *Self-perceived attractiveness* is also positively correlated with nontraditional career practices.

(*E13*)   *Self-perceived height* is positively correlated with nontraditional career status; *tall* women are most likely to be career-oriented.

(*E14*)   *Self-perceived strength* is positively associated with nontraditional career development.

This literature suggests that several background variables which themselves deviate from normative expectations have facilitated women breaking through normative sets to enter nontraditional careers. For example, being reared by mothers who themselves model nonconforming behaviors by being employed, particularly in nontraditional careers, seems to be important for nontraditional career development. Encouragement from other nontraditional women in support groups or as role models in college and post-college training also seems important for pioneer career development. Membership in a minority religion, Jewish or Unitarian, has a positive relationship to nontraditional career status. In addition, these women consider themselves brighter, more attractive, taller and stronger than other women. The combination of a nontraditional career status with a nonnormative background leads one to question whether these women are presently leading atypical lives. Nontraditional career women, are in fact, single more often than other women, a marital status which is presently nonconforming for adult women in America. Thus, the literature depicts nontraditional career women as generally nonnormative—they experienced a nonnormative background, have assumed a nontraditional career status, and may be presently leading nonconforming lives.

Critique of the Literature

Although the relationships between background variables and career orientation of women have been researched for the last decade, few if any conclusions can be made from the findings because the studies are methodologically weak and the findings scattered. Virtually all of these studies attempting to correlate specific conditions with pioneer professional status are based on projections of high school, college (most often in an introductory psychology or sociology course) and graduate student women. There is in fact almost no research exploring these factors with women who have actually entered their nontraditional career (Lemkau, 1979; Steinberg, 1976; Connolly, Burks & Rogers, 1976; Theodore, 1971).

At present it is very difficult to predict actual achievements of women from projected plans (Harmon, 1981, 1970; Card, Steel & Abeles, 1980; Safilios-Rothschild, 1979). The available research demonstrates that in spite of the recent rise in stated aspirational levels, there has not been the same increase in women's overall occupational status (Robinowitz et al., 1981; Walles et al., 1981; Newsweek, 1976). In fact, there has been a progressive decrease in the ratio of women to men as educational or professional status increases; i.e., in 1972, 43% of bachelor's degrees earned went to women, whereas only 40% of all master's degrees, 14% of all doctorate degrees and 6% of all professional degrees were granted to women (Angrist & Almquist, 1975; Randour et al., 1982).

Research by Astin and Panos (1969) & Harmon (1981) found that during the college years, women who had initially named a "masculine" career choice were likely to switch to a more "feminine" field (especially teaching and paraprofessional health careers) and were unlikely to actualize their original "masculine" career choice. Other research examining the persistence of career goals in high school and/or college women during a four to five year period (Lentz, 1982 a & b; Astin, 1968a, 1968b; Almquist & Angrist, 1971) suggest that interests, intelligence and abilities in high school can predict certain college career choices. Comparisons between traditional and nontraditional career goals or level of degree (e.g., bachelor or graduate degree) were not made, however. In light of these findings, it is not clear whether women's actualized career behaviors have or will change as much as their projected goals. Clearly, then, the research findings illustrate the problem of identifying supportive background conditions for professional women when the information is limited to projections of career-oriented women.

A number of other methodological problems also exist with this research. The measurements used in different studies are very diverse and are based on different criteria for defining career-orientation. In some instances, the variables being correlated (e.g., degree of creativity, enterprising) are too vaguely defined to provide any clear meaning for further evaluations. In some studies implicit assumptions are made about the subjects without research to support the assumptions. For example, nontraditional career-oriented women are consistently tested and analyzed together without research to document that different groups of nontraditional women (e.g., doctors, lawyers, academicians, scientists) are in fact statistically alike. The almost nonexistence of studies using national, longitudinal, cross-sectional or cross-professional comparisons has also resulted in limited generalizability.

Overview

Existing research is not adequate to provide reliable or valid information about background variables affecting women's career choices. Instead of asking young women about their career plans, as most previous studies have done, this study asked women who had already entered careers about their background. Such information seems essential if we, as individuals, professionals or groups are to encourage environments supportive of a wider range of career choices by women.

The study was designed to systematically examine the relationship between the status of nontraditional professional woman and a) employment background; b) educational background; c) family and demographic background (e.g., parents' education and occupation, religious upbringing, birth order, family size, childhood interests, childhood relationships with parents); d) self-characteristic variables of attractiveness, intelligence, height and strength; e) environmental variables (e.g., marital status, closest friends, hobbies); and f) significant others and significant events influencing the woman's life/career choices. The main focus of the investigation was on behaviors and environmental conditions rather than on attitudes or feelings, because there is little evidence that these subjective factors have systematic impact on career development.

As noted, many of these variables had been reviewed in previous studies using career-oriented women. Because of the shortcomings found in the existing literature, particularly the problems of the limited subject populations used, projective procedures, and the contradictory and inconclusive evidence generated, the present study explored these same issues as well as others collected in a pilot study, comparing women with a variety of career statuses. From the pilot studies, an instrument was developed and tested with women who have become either nontraditional career women (doctors and lawyers), traditional career women (home economists and nurses) or homemakers.

In sum, the goals of this study were to: 1) Examine if there are patterns of variables that differentiate the background and current lifestyle of contemporary women who have chosen: a) nontraditional careers, traditional careers, or homemaking, and b) particular professions. In particular, this study will explore the patterns most closely associated with nontraditional career status to determine if they differ substantially from normative expectations of women's behaviors in American culture. 2) Examine the validity of previous findings by studying women who have already entered careers, rather than testing women who expect to enter careers as in most previous research.

2

Method

Sample

The total sample included 309 women residing/practicing in Colorado or Ohio: 57 doctors who are members of the American Medical Women's Assoc., Inc.; 47 lawyers; 64 home economists who are members of the Colorado or Ohio Home Economics Assoc.; 60 public health nurses; and 81 homemakers with at least some college education (85% had earned at least bachelor degrees). Another 22 completed questionnaires were returned which were excluded from analysis for various reasons (one lawyer's questionnaire was completed by a man; one lawyer, one nurse and one homemaker returned their questionnaires too late to be analyzed; 14 homemakers were employed more than just a few hours/week and could not be classified as full-time homemakers; four homemakers' questionnaires were completed by the daughters of the homemakers and not the homemakers themselves). In addition, seven questionnaires were returned with explanations as to why the woman was choosing not to participate in the study (two lawyers did not have the time; one lawyer felt she had been in too many previous studies; one homemaker and one home economist were in the midst of divorces; one doctor and one home economist were no longer employed at the addresses where the questionnaires were sent). Table 1 presents the mean and modal age for each of the five groups of women. These women ranged in age from 23 to 86 with homemakers and doctors being the oldest group and nurses the youngest group sampled.

The 200 nontraditional women were randomly selected from two listings: All Colorado and Ohio women doctors who were members of the American Medical Women's Assoc. Inc. and courthouse listings of all registered lawyers in Colorado and Ohio. The second category of women, the traditional career women, were randomly chosen from two listings: members of the Colorado and Ohio Economics Associations and employees of the Denver and Columbus Public Health Nurses Association. All of the traditional career women had earned at least college level degrees. The last category, the homemakers, consisted of women randomly selected who were married to professionals (faculty wives and Junior Women's Club Members) who did not fit into either category one or two, and who had at least some college education.

Table 1.   Mean and Modal Age of the Five
Groups of Women (N = 309)

Group	N	Mean Age	Modal Age
Home Economists	64	41	41
Doctors	57	50	34
Lawyers	47	36	28–30
Homemakers	81	46	46
Nurses	60	31	31

Instruments

The questionnaire utilized (Appendix A) was developed through a series of three pilot studies since the existing literature on the backgrounds of professional women (especially nontraditional women) is sparse and unreliable. In the first pilot study, 10 nontraditional women were informally interviewed to help select relevant questions for a larger study. The informal interviews supported the idea that some of the factors previously discovered as well as some new ones have been influential in women's nontraditional career development. For example, a few of the academicians and medical women questioned stated that an encouraging and supportive professor was critical in helping them persist with their desired goals. Working in a variety of unsatisfactory jobs in order to financially support their education was also offered as a reason why some of these women persevered to become professionals. Family situations demonstrating the possibility that women may have to work to support themselves as well as their families (e.g., death, divorce) encouraged a few women to pursue their careers.

Once a questionnaire was developed combining past research instruments with the new ideas generated in this first pilot, another pilot study was implemented. In this pilot study, 15 Colorado women, five from each career category, responded to a cover letter and questionnaire in order to determine the clarity of the instruments and the time involved in responding. The researcher then met with each woman to discuss her answers and any problems she encountered regarding the instruments. Suggestions from this pilot were incorporated into a second form of the questionnaire. A third pilot using the revised instrument and following the same procedure as the previous pilot resulted in sufficient diversity and clarity in the questions to warrant the instruments being used in the full-scale study.

The questionnaire, which took approximately 15–30 minutes to complete, was designed to elicit information on some demographic and family background variables, self-perception variables, employment background variables, and academic environmental variables.

In Part I, subjects were asked to respond to a close-ended questionnaire in order to provide personal background data. In Part II, subjects were asked to respond to 42 5-point Likert-type items which referred to variables associated with career-orientation. Part III, the open-ended portion of the questionnaire, was designed to elaborate on some of the information concerning previous variables suggested as well as elicit any new variables which pioneer career women support as having positively affected their professional development.

Procedure

In an attempt to gain the support of the women, a letter (Appendix B) personally addressed to each woman detailing the rationale and goals of the study as well as offering the option to receive a copy of the results was mailed along with the questionnaire to 600 women (200/category; 300 in Colorado and 300 in Ohio). Envelopes stamped and addressed to the author were also sent along with the questionnaires. Each questionnaire had a numerical coding which was destroyed once the questionnaire was returned and all the data was computer recorded. These codings were used because they enabled subjects' responses to remain anonymous while also enabling the researcher to monitor questionnaire returns (Babbie, 1973). The response rate for useable and nonuseable questionnaires ranged from 37% to 58%, averaging 48% return rate for questionnaires.

In an attempt to assess the extent to which responders were similar to nonresponders, 10 percent of the women who did not respond to the mailed questionnaire were randomly chosen and called by the author. These women were asked to respond on the phone to a subset of the questions (Appendix C) on the full questionnaire. This short phone interview included mostly questions asking for demographic data; demographic data is most commonly used with surveys and seems like the most efficient and useful data to collect in a short telephone conversation for comparison purposes. A few other questions relating to participation in women's groups and commitment to marital/career situation were also asked because of their relevance to the study. In order to obtain the necessary 10% (36 responders), 39 women were called; two lawyers and one homemaker refused to answer the phone questionnaire. The response rate for phone questionnaires was 92%.

In order to assess the efficacy and validity of the questionnaire as an instrument, a subsample of 40 women living either in Denver, Boulder, or Fort Collins, Colorado or Columbus, Ohio were interviewed in person by the author. Twenty-five women/category living in these four cities were randomly chosen to be interviewed instead of mailed the questionnaire; the first 12–14 accepting/category were interviewed. During these sessions, the author read the questionnaire to the subject and recorded the woman's answer. In order to interview 40 women, 45 women were called (one doctor, one lawyer, one nurse and three homemakers refused to participate in the interview). The response rate for interviewees was 89%.

Analyses

The aim of the analysis was to determine: 1) if the five groups of professional women/three categories of career women were different; 2) if there were any patterns or categories of variables which differentiated the groups of women; and 3) if the three types of responses, i.e., questionnaire, phone interview, and face-to-face interview, made any difference on the answers given. In other words, could the different groups of women (particularly the nontraditional career women) be described by a specific set of items; and in addition, could these items fit into a particular framework (e.g., psychological, sociological, ecological). The analysis was an attempt to describe the women's perceptions of influential background variables and was not an attempt to accurately determine the extent to which each variable played a significant role in the women's career development.

The sample was analyzed in terms of: 1) the five occupational groups of doctors, lawyers, home economists, nurses and homemakers; 2) the three career categories of nontraditional career women (N = 101), traditional career women (N = 124) and homemakers (N = 81); and 3) the three types of responses of 233 mailed questionnaires (doctors = 43, lawyers = 33, home economists = 52, nurses = 47, homemakers = 58), 40 face-to-face interviews (doctors = 7, lawyers = 7, home economists = 7, nurses = 7, homemakers = 12) and 36 phone interviews (doctors = 7, lawyers = 7, home economists = 5, nurses = 6, homemakers = 11).

A coding manual for the questionnaire was developed (Appendix D). For those questions with precategorized answers (e.g., religious background: Agnostic, Atheist, Catholic, Jewish, Protestant, Unitarian, Other), numerical codes corresponding to the answer were devised. For those more open questions without pre-determined categories (e.g., Hobbies _____), answers from samples of approximately 75–100 questionnaires were recorded, categorized and coded. To insure consistency of coding, all responses designated to a specific numerical category were recorded in the coding manual.

The principal analyses used with this coded questionnaire data were chi-square, MANOVA (Multiple Analysis of Variance), factor analysis, multiple regression analyses, and content analysis. Chi-square comparisons were used to compare: (1) the five groups of professional women; (2) the three categories of career women; (3) doctors with lawyers; and (4) home economists with nurses in terms of the background variables found in Part I of the questionnaire.

MANOVAs were used to compare the five groups of women to see if the groups differed significantly from each other on four subsamples (employment, education, family and environment/self) of these personal background variables. In the MANOVA procedures, the test of significance employed was the Wilk's lambda criterion. The approximate F cited was derived using Rao's approximation. Because the MANOVA had four degrees of freedom, a maximum of four a priori MANOVA comparisons could be conducted. The four comparisons chosen and analyzed because they were the most relevant to the hypotheses being tested were: (1) all professionals vs. homemakers; (2) nontraditional vs. traditional career categories; (3) doctors vs. lawyers; and (4) home economists with nurses. The variables included in these analyses met two criteria: 1) their content was relevant to the subsample being analyzed; and 2) data on the variable was available from most of the subjects sampled.

Factor analysis using the principal axis method with the squared multiple correlation as the estimate for communality was performed on the 42 Likert-scaled variables (in the second portion of the questionnaire) in order to determine if any of these items clustered. The factors were rotated to orthogonal simple structure by the varimax procedure. The least squares method was used to estimate subjects' scores on the rotated factors since this method is most appropriate when investigating group differences on factor scores (Tucker, 1971). Factor analyses computed with and without missing data were very similar; the factor analysis without missing data was used. Ten orthogonal factors were chosen because the 10 factors accounted for the majority of the estimated common variance (98%) and extraction of additional factors did not appear justified. In addition, orthogonal factors were chosen because oblique factor pattern matrices were very similar to the orthogonal pattern and intercorrelations between factors were too small to warrant attention. These 10 factors accounted for 43% of the total variance. Salient loadings of variables on the factors were defined as loadings greater than or equal to $|.30|$. In the following information, only the salient loadings will be listed. Table 2 presents the 10 factors with their associated items, factor loadings and percent of the total variance they accounted for.

Factor 1: Positive Self-Image as a Child. Seven items loaded highly on this factor. All of the items included on the factor seem to reflect a child's image of herself as positive. Only the variable, confidence, which does not necessarily reflect a positive self-image as a child, is found on another factor (Factor 8). None of the 35 other variables included in the factor analysis seem to reflect a positive self-image as a child. Thus, this factor seemed to cluster all the items which belong to it.

Table 2. Ten Factors With Their Associated Items, Factor Loadings and Percent of the Total Variance They Accounted For

Factor	Item	Factor Loading	Percent of Total Variance Accounted For
1. Positive Self-Image as a Child	As a child: assertive	.766	6.6%
	As a child: self-confident	.687	
	As a child: independent	.657	
	As a child: competitive	.591	
	As a child: friendly and outgoing	.564	
	Presently: confident	.365	
	In high school, kept company with many people	.298	
2. Positive Orientation Towards Marriage and Children	During adolescence, strong thoughts and commitment to marriage	.816	6.9%
	During adolescence, strong thoughts and commitment to children	.853	
	During college, strong thoughts and commitment to marriage	.771	
	During college, strong thoughts and commitment to children	.788	
3. Mother's Non-employment	Mother was not employed	.869	4.0%
	Mother was employed	-.877	
4. Nontraditional Career Orientation	During high school, strong interests and commitment to nontraditional career	.737	6.0%
	During college, strong interests and commitment to nontraditional career	.785	
	During high school, strong interests and commitment to traditional career	-.714	
	During college, strong interests and commitment to traditional career	-.688	

Table 2. (Continued)

Factor	Item	Factor Loading	Percent of Total Variance Accounted For
	Presently: intelligent	.307	
5. Participation in Volunteer Groups	Member: Voluntary Service Group	.519	3.9%
	Member: Social Group	.562	
	Member: Religious Group	.463	
	Member: Auxilliary Group	.579	
	Positive effects on career development	-.373	
6. Negative Relationship with Parents	Relationship with father as a child was positive	-.622	4.0%
	Relationship with mother as a child was positive	-.590	
	Relationship with father is positive	-.539	
	Relationship with mother is positive	-.575	
7. Political Activism	Membership: Moderate Feminist Group	.71	3.4%
	Membership: Political Group	.65	
	Intelligence	.33	
8. (Present) Positive Self-Image	Strong	.464	3.0%
	Attractive	.441	
	Intelligent	.413	
	Confident	.493	
	Tall	.368	
9. Sex Appropriate Orientation	As a child, I was feminine	.459	2.5%
	As a child, I played with girls	.486	
	As a child, I recall unhappy experiences	.371	
10. Self-Discipline and Planning	Positive effects of employment history	.467	2.3%
	Planning involved in employment history	.394	
	As a child, I did as parents told me	.305	

Factor 2: Positive Orientation Towards Marriage and Children. Four items loaded highly on this factor. All of the items included on the factor seem to involve a positive trend towards marriage and children. None of these four items are found in any of the other nine factors. And, none of the other 38 variables in the factor analysis seem to reflect a positive orientation towards motherhood. Thus, this factor seems to involve all and only all the items which belong with it.

Factor 3: Mother's Non-employment. Only two items loaded highly on this factor. Because only two items are involved with this factor, this factor is a doublet and is not very interesting. In addition, the factor loadings of the two variables are in opposite directions; this is expected since the items involved are mutually exclusive of each other and should be highly correlated in opposite directions. Factor 3 therefore does not add much information to the analysis.

Factor 4: Nontraditional Career Orientation. Five items loaded highly on this factor. Four of the items included on the factor seem to reflect a trend towards a career in which women do not often enter. Only the variable, intelligence, which does not necessarily imply a nontraditional career orientation, is found on another factor (#7 and #8). None of the other 37 variables included in the factor analysis seem to reflect a nontraditional career orientation. Thus, Factor 4 seemed to cluster all the items which belong to it.

Factor 5: Participation in Volunteer Groups. Five items loaded highly on this factor. Four of the items included on this factor seem to involve participation in volunteer groups. Only the variable discussing the effects of this participation on career development does not necessarily imply participation in volunteer groups. None of these items are found on any of the other factors. Only one of the other 37 variables included in the factor analysis, Member: League of Women Voters, seems to reflect volunteer groups. This factor seemed to cluster most of the items which belong to it.

Factor 6: Negative Relationship with Parents. Four variables loaded highly on this factor. All of the items included on the factor seem to discuss perceptions of the relationship with one's parents as negative. None of these items are found on any of the other nine factors. In addition, none of the other 38 variables included in the factor analysis seem to relate to the relationship with one's parents. Thus, the factor seemed to cluster all and only all the items which belong to it.

Factor 7: Political Activism. Three items loaded highly on this factor. The first two items included on the factor seem to reflect involvement in political groups; this factor is therefore almost a doublet. Only the variable, intelligence, which does not necessarily imply political activism is found on another factor (#4 and #8). None of the other 39 variables included in the factor analysis seem to reflect political activity. Thus, Factor 7 seemed to cluster all the items which belong to it.

Factor 8: (Present) Positive Self-Image. Five items loaded highly on this factor. All of the items included on the factor seem to reflect a positive self-image. Two of the items, intelligence and confidence, are found on other factors (#4 and #7, #1 respectively). None of the other 37 variables included in the factor analysis seem to belong in the Positive Self-Image cluster. Thus, Factor 8 seemed to include all the items which belong to it.

Factor 9: Sex Appropriate Orientation. Three items loaded highly on this factor. The first two items in the factor seem to suggest sex appropriate behaviors as a child; this factor is therefore almost a doublet. None of the items are found on any other of the nine factors. In addition, none of the other 39 variables seem to reflect a sex appropriate orientation as a child. Thus, Factor 9 seemed to cluster all the items which belong to it.

Factor 10: Self-Discipline and Planning. Three items loaded highly on this factor. All of the items seem to relate to disciplining oneself and planning. None of the items are found on any of the other nine factors and none of the other 39 variables in the factor analysis seem to relate to self-discipline and planning. Thus, this factor seemed to include all and only all the items which belong to it.

In addition to these ten factors, separate clusters of items (child-assertive, child-self-confident, child-independent, child-competitive, child-friendly; relationship with mother was, relationship with mother is, relationship with father was, relationship with father is; high school career thoughts were traditional, high school career thoughts were nontraditional, college career thoughts were traditional, college career thoughts were nontraditional, adolescent thoughts were towards marriage, adolescent thoughts were towards children, in college was married, in college had children) were checked for multidimensionality. The findings demonstrated that only one factor could be justified for each cluster.

A MANOVA with the above mentioned four a priori comparisons was performed using the ten factor scores as dependent variables to determine if the five groups of individuals differed significantly from each other on these clustered variables. Multiple regression analyses using the ten factor scores as criteria and a subsample of the background variables as predictors (detailed in Appendix E) were made to assess the extent to which some of the variables being analyzed in the first part of the questionnaire could predict variables in the second part of the questionnaire.

Primarily results which were significant at the .05 level are reported. Trend differences, results near the .05 level, are also reported when they are supportive of results which were significant at the .05 level or better.

The open-ended questions from the third part of the questionnaire were analyzed for frequencies of responses by the following procedure: 1) all responses from all of the subjects were recorded; 2) these answers were summarized and outlined according to four main categories of responses (employment and related events, significant events which were not employment related, significant person variables, and self-variables—listed in Appendix F); and 3) all subjects responses were coded, counted and averaged according to the four categories. Where illustrative, direct quotes will be presented.

3

Results

The results are reported in terms of five sets of variables: employment and related events, education, family, environment, and self. For each of these sets, data are reported comparing the five groups of professional women (doctors, lawyers, home economists, nurses and homemakers) and three categories of career women (nontraditional, traditional, and homemakers). The data are presented in the same order as it appeared in the questionnaire. (The total list of responses and associated frequencies given to open-ended questions is listed in Appendix F.) Summaries for each set of data will primarily be concerned with statistically significant differences among the five professional groups of women. Following presentations of the results for the total sample, within career category comparisons (doctors with lawyers and home economists with nurses) will be presented. The analysis of the data in terms of the three types of responses (questionnaire, short phone interview and longer face-to-face interview) resulted in very few significant differences between the groups. This finding justified pooling all of the data for the analyses reported here. However, in those few cases where significant differences were obtained among the different types of responses, the data will be reported (e.g., see Tables 3, 5, 9, 14, and 20). In addition, the similarity of results obtained from the various response methods supports the validity of the questionnaire as well as the representativeness of the sample.

Briefly, many significant differences between the groups are suggested by the data. Tables 3 and 4 present the results of F tests from MANOVAs on five professional groups by face-to-face interview and questionnaire responses on 10 factors (derived from Likert-type attitudinal variables asking the women to compare themselves with other women on various life situations, e.g., Factor 1: Positive Self-Image as a Child, Factor 2: Positive Orientation Towards Marriage and Children). As shown in Tables 3 and 4, there was an overall significant difference, $p < .001$, among the five groups of women in terms of the factors. These same tables show that in category by factor MANOVAs of this data, all professionals were different from homemakers, $F(10,254) = 16.20, p < .001$, and nontraditional women were different from traditional women, $F(10,254) = 28.77, p < .001$. Because the various analyses presented

Table 3. Results of F tests from MANOVAs on Five Professional
Groups By Face-to-Face Interview and Questionnaire
Responses on 10 Factors

Source	Variable	DFHYP/DFERR	MSHYP/MSERR	F
Group		40/964		11.09*
(Doctors, lawyers, home econ-	Factor 1: Positive self-image as a child	4/263	2.598/1.215	2.14
omists, nurses, home- makers)	Factor 2: Positive orientation towards marriage & children	4/263	2.123/1.103	1.93
	Factor 3: Mother's non-employment	4/263	1.026/1.163	.88
	Factor 4: Nontraditional career orientation	4/263	37.655/0.667	56.44*
	Factor 5: Participation in voluntary groups	4/263	25.027/1.163	21.52*
	Factor 6: Negative relationship with parents	4/263	2.566/1.388	1.85
	Factor 7: Political activism	4/263	8.310/1.424	5.83*
	Factor 8: (Present) positive self image	4/263	3.043/1.532	1.99
	Factor 9: Sex appropriate orientation	4/263	11.687/1.450	8.06*
	Factor 10: Self-discipline and planning	4/263	1.288/1.776	.73
Response (Question- naire, Interview)		10/254		1.82
Group X Response interaction		40/964		.68

*$p < .001$

Table 4. Means and Standard Deviations of 10 Factors by Five
Professional Groups

Factors		Home Economists	Doctors	Lawyers	Homemakers	Nurses
Factor 1:	M	.112	.197	.207	-.032	-.337
	SD	1.012	1.137	1.104	1.174	1.104
	N	60	50	40	70	53
Factor 2:	M	-.162	-.224	-.156	.186	.147
	SD	1.074	1.042	1.005	1.096	1.040
	N	60	50	40	70	53
Factor 3:	M	.014	-.069	-.045	.184	-.163
	SD	.999	1.092	1.141	1.110	1.069
	N	60	50	40	70	53
Factor 4:	M	-.791	1.160	.822	-.251	-.522
	SD	.772	.808	.892	.890	.702
	N	60	50	40	70	53
Factor 5:	M	-.095	-.283	-.416	.973	-.651
	SD	1.027	1.022	1.009	1.189	1.037
	N	60	50	40	70	53
Factor 6:	M	-.128	-.272	.370	.036	-.060
	SD	1.326	1.284	1.170	1.084	.992
	N	60	50	40	70	53
Factor 7:	M	.106	-.154	.790	-.268	-.165
	SD	1.093	1.196	1.996	.640	1.029
	N	60	50	40	70	53
Factor 8:	M	.055	-.045	.469	-.097	-.214
	SD	1.035	1.228	1.369	1.376	1.132
	N	60	50	40	70	53
Factor 9:	M	.263	.751	-.256	-.409	-.089
	SD	1.181	1.378	1.280	1.075	1.147
	N	60	50	40	70	53
Factor 10:	M	-.087	.264	-.134	-.003	-.100
	SD	1.315	1.264	1.263	1.441	1.290
	N	60	50	40	70	53

throughout the results chapter show that there are more significant differences when the data* is analyzed in terms of the five professional groups, doctor, lawyer, nurse, home economist and homemaker, than when the data is analyzed in terms of the three career categories, nontraditional, traditional and homemaker, a second presentation of the data (following the total sample presentation) focusing on a comparison of doctors with lawyers and home economists with nurses is warranted.

Professional Group Differences

Employment and Related Variables

The variables analyzed in the employment subgroup include the subjects' time employed in the present position, the number of jobs she held and the fields the jobs were in after high school, the number of jobs held during high school, reasons for leaving these various employment positions, participation in volunteer groups (Factor 5), political activism (Factor 7), and various responses given in the open-ended portion of the questionnaire (e.g., positive and negative occupational role models, positive and negative career encouragement from significant others, characteristics of the job).

Tables 5 and 6 show that a MANOVA of all five of the professional groups with three work variables (jobs after high school, fields jobs were in, jobs in high school) resulted in a significant overall group difference, $p < .001$. The MANOVA contrasting the five groups of women in terms of the three types of responses on the work variables also resulted in a significant finding, $p < .013$.

Figure 1 shows that a chi square of the four groups of professional women** comparing their time employed in the present position resulted in substantial differences between these groups, $X^2(9) = 23.41, p < .005$. Home economists and doctors had been employed the longest in their present positions, at least six years, lawyers next (modal response = 2–3 years) and nurses the least amount of time with less than one year as their modal response.

Referring back to Tables 5 and 6, the MANOVA comparing all professionals with homemakers in terms of the number of jobs after high school resulted in a significant difference, $F(1,289) = 21.19, p < .001$, with the professionals having held more jobs. The home economists had the highest

---

* In surveys, the word data is used as a collective noun. Even though grammatically incorrect, useage of data has evolved and will be used in this study with singular verbs.

** Homemakers, who are by the definition used in this research not employed outside of the home, were excluded from this analysis.

Table 5. Results of F Tests from MANOVAs on Five Professional Groups by Questionnaire, Phone Interview and Face-to-Face Interview Responses on Three Work Variables

Source	Variable	DFHYP/DFERR	MSHYP/MSERR	F
Group		12/764		5.37**
(Home Econ- omists,	No. Jobs After High School	4/291	21.855/3.630	6.02**
Doctors, Lawyers,	No. Fields Jobs Were In	4/291	8.488/1.718	4.94**
Home- makers, Nurses)	No. Jobs in High School	4/291	2.341/1.191	1.97
Response		6/578		2.73*
(Question naire,	No. Jobs After High School	2/291	12.069/3.630	3.33*
Mini-phone interview,	No. Fields Jobs Were In	2/291	2.912/1.718	1.70
Face-to- face inter- view)	No. Jobs in High School	2/291	4.601/1.191	3.86*
Group X Response Inter- action		24/838		1.17

*$p < .05$
**$p < .001$

number of jobs after high school, mean $= 4.4$, followed by the lawyers, doctors, nurses and then the homemakers, mean $= 2.9$. When looking at post high school jobs in terms of the fields they were in, the ANOVA suggests a trend for homemakers' jobs to have been in a greater variety of fields than those of the professional women's, $F(1,291) = 3.72$, $p < .055$. Among the career women, the nontraditional professionals held jobs in a greater variety of fields than the traditional ones, $F(1,291) = 7.71, p < .006$. Lawyers reported having the most jobs in high school (mode $= 3$, mean $= 1.5$) while home economists reported having the least (mode $= 0$, mean $= .92$) number of jobs of all five groups although the overall five group ANOVA for high school jobs was not statistically significant. The telephone mini-questionnaire subjects reported significantly more, $F(1,291) = 7.67$, $p < .006$, high school jobs than the questionnaire or interview responders.

In addition to information about the number of jobs, information about reasons for leaving jobs was also collected. A large number of reasons for

Table 6. Means and Standard Deviations of Three Work Variables by
Five Professional Groups

Work Variable		Home Economists	Doctors	Lawyers	Homemakers	Nurses
No. Jobs After High School	M	4.369	3.909	4.04	2.925	3.864
	SD	1.957	2.254	2.063	1.744	1.726
	N	65	55	47	81	59
No. Fields Jobs Were In	M	1.630	1.636	2.212	1.962	1.186
	SD	1.153	1.495	1.249	1.661	.706
	N	65	55	47	81	59
No. Jobs in High School	M	.921	1.036	1.489	1.111	1.084
	SD	.878	1.121	1.457	1.012	1.087
	N	64	55	47	81	59

Figure 1: Time Employed with Present Employer by Four
Professional Groups.
(N = 212, $p < .005$)

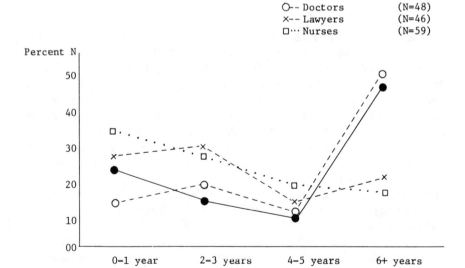

Legend

●— Home Economists (N=59)
○-- Doctors   (N=48)
✕-- Lawyers   (N=46)
□⋯ Nurses   (N=59)

leaving a job were given (listed in Appendix D); of the 17 which were coded and analyzed, seven of these resulted in significant differences. Table 7 presents the results of women's reasons for leaving a job. "Moving" was most often cited by the traditional women and least often by the nontraditional women in the five-group, $p < .007$, and three-category, $X^2(2) = 12.28, p < .002$, analyses; 38% of the traditional women reported "moving" while only 18% of the nontraditional women claimed "moving" as a reason for leaving their job. The traditional women also reported leaving for a "more desirable position" the most and homemakers the least in the five-way, $p < .0001$, and three-way, $X^2(2) = 26.99, p < .0001$, analyses. Fifty-eight percent of the traditional women but only 18% of the homemakers reported "more desirable position" as a reason for leaving. "Dissatisfaction with job" was reported as a reason for leaving jobs by 20% of the women; nurses reported this most (45%) with the home economists least (5%), $p < .0001$. For example, one nurse explains, "Unfortunately nurses take a lot of grief from doctors and others. I have found this intolerable in most cases and feel that the reason is that nursing has been traditionally female. For this reason I am seriously considering changing professions." The comparison of "dissatisfaction with job" by women's career categories, traditional, nontraditional and homemaker, was not significant.

In response to open-ended questions, doctors (9 references) and home economists (9 references), more than the other three groups stated that they left their jobs for "higher education" or because their "previous jobs were not rewarding enough." Homemakers (3 responses) reported this reason far less frequently than any of the four professional groups. The results of the chi square with the five groups, $p < .0001$, and three categories, $X^2(2) = 6.66, p < .035$, for the reason "more school" were similar to these open-ended results with 41% of the home economists giving this reason and the others giving this reason 24% or less frequently. "Marriage," on the other hand, in the five group, $p < .001$, and three group, $X^2(2) = 37.12, p < .001$, analysis was most often cited by homemakers (35%), occasionally by home economists (12%) and rarely by others. One homemaker's response illustrates how marriage affected her career, "I'd planned on a Ph.D. in Family Life Education but my marriage to an older man who did and does not want me out of the home for schooling or employment changed that. It took him 6 months to realize my intent then boom! I was home." Doctors never reported "marriage" as a reason for leaving a job. "Children, pregnancy, and family" in the five-group, $p < .001$, and three-category, $X^2(2) = 20.02, p < .0001$, analyses was again most often claimed by homemakers (43%), followed by lawyers (29%); the others gave this reason 18% of the time or less (Table 8). Again quoting a homemaker, "At the time I expected to return to school later, but when I did so when our older two children were 3 and 1 1/2, it quickly became apparent that any education on my part was to be over and above my regular duties as

Table 7. Reasons for Leaving a Job by Five Professional Groups

Reason for Leaving a Job	Home Economists Percent No	Yes	N	Doctors Percent No	Yes	N	Lawyers Percent No	Yes	N	Homemakers Percent No	Yes	N	Nurses Percent No	Yes	N	Total Percent No	Yes	N
Moving $X^2(24) = 14.04$, $p < .007$	68%	32%	56	85%	15%	41	79%	21%	34	57%	43%	65	57%	43%	51	67%	33%	247
More Desirable Position $X^2(4) = 30.63$, $p < .001$	45%	55%	55	56%	44%	41	76%	24%	34	82%	18%	65	39%	61%	51	60%	40%	246
Dissatisfaction with the Job $X^2(4) = 31.52$, $p < .001$	95%	5%	56	93%	7%	41	79%	21%	34	78%	21%	65	55%	45%	51	80%	20%	247
More School $X^2(4) = 25.38$, $p < .001$	59%	41%	56	80%	20%	41	76%	24%	34	91%	9%	65	92%	8%	51	80%	20%	247
Marriage $X^2(4) = 38.24$, $p < .001$	88%	12%	56	100%	0%	41	97%	3%	34	65%	35%	35	94%	6%	51	86%	14%	247
Pregnancy, Children and/or Family $X^2(4) = 25.69$, $p < .001$	82%	18%	56	93%	7%	41	71%	29%	34	57%	43%	65	88%	12%	51	77%	23%	247
Position was Held in Conjunction with Earning a Degree $X^2(4) = 33.14$, $p < .001$	86%	14%	56	68%	32%	41	91%	9%	34	98%	2%	65	100%	0%	51	90%	10%	247

Table 8. Background Variables Which Predict Participation in
Volunteer Groups (Factor 5) (N = 309)

Source	Beta	F Value	Probability
Homemaker	+	63.92	.0001
Age	+	34.47	.0001

Note. $F(2,306) = 63.04$, $p < .0001$

wife and mother. There were never so many complaints about my housekeeping, nor so much reluctance to help at home, as then. After one year I decided the hassle wasn't worth it, quit, and had two more children which I probably wouldn't have if I had been working. Now the die is cast." Of the 10% of the women who reported leaving because the "position was held in conjunction with earning a degree," doctors (32%) reported this much more often than the other groups with nurses never citing this reason in the five-way analysis, $p < .001$.

In the open-ended section of the questionnaire, women discussed their employment history and how it affected their career development. "Previous job experiences positively influenced my career" was most often mentioned by the traditional women (42 references) and least often by the nontraditional women (18 references). Understood in this question is the homemakers' response that previous employment reinforced their decision to become homemakers. To illustrate the effects of previous employment, one nurse responded by writing, "Jobs I worked to get spending money through college etc. were *HORRID* to think of as life long—waitress, paper, aides in hospital. I knew I better find a more rewarding way to support myself." Quoting another nurse, "Really it began in high school—when I wanted to go with the group to study in Scotland, but we didn't have the money—mom said if I worked for the money I could go. And I did! And I've continued to enjoy working and earning my own money." Homemakers (9 references) most often reported "previous job experiences which deterred them from future employment"—"The jobs I got were always to get by—I didn't think in terms of career advancement. Mostly I have done boring parttime work, during school. *I wish I had had some models for career planning* . . . now it is hard for me to consider pursuing a career." Traditional women were next with a total of seven references and the nontraditional women almost never reported negative previous job experiences.

"Characteristics of the jobs" such as "ability to work 9 a.m. to 5 p.m. and integrate work and family life, prestige, ability to afford material comforts, or challenging" were most often reported by nurses (33 responses) as reasons for desiring their career. Lawyers were second and home economists last (7 responses). No explanation or discussion of employment history was given when the responder wrote "I have always wanted to be in this profession." Doctors (23 references) reported this "always wanted to be" phenomena the most; homemakers and home economists followed them closely with nurses (14 references) and lawyers (12 references) reporting this idea less than the other groups.

Three different analyses show that homemakers participate in volunteer groups more than the other groups of women. Data taken from Tables 3 and 4 show that an ANOVA of Factor 5—"Participation in Volunteer Groups"—found that homemakers were significantly different from all professionals on their level of involvement in volunteer groups, $F(1,263) = 78.24$, $p < .001$. Table 8 indicates that regression analysis shows that 22.3% of the variance of this factor could be accounted for by the homemaker group, and the older the homemaker the more likely she would be involved in volunteer groups (age accounts for the next 9.5% of the variance, $p < .0001$ as shown in Table 8). The benefits of volunteer work, particularly in the League of Women Voters, was also cited in the open-ended questions most often by the homemakers (5 references); the nontraditional women almost never referred to volunteer groups.

Tables 3 and 4 show that an ANOVA of "political activism" (Factor 7) indicates that all professionals are involved more than homemakers, $F(1,263) = 5.10$, $p < .025$. Data from these same tables show that another ANOVA comparing nontraditionals with traditionals, however, only suggests that nontraditional women's political participation is somewhat greater than that of traditional women, $F(1,263) = 2.89$, $p < .090$. In the open-ended section, only lawyers reported supportive experiences coming from their participation in these women's political groups.

Participation in women's support groups also received reactions from women. Three other nontraditional women reported their appreciation of their support groups for having helped them deal with "male chauvinist" colleagues. In direct contrast to these positive reactions to participation in all women's groups, however, several subjects suggested that they find all women's groups a waste of their time. One lawyer responded "I join groups to add to my career, not to be segregated."

The open-ended responses also suggest that "positive encouragement from a non-relative, employment-related significant person" most positively influenced the traditional women (17 references) with their career development. Lawyers (3 references) reported this encouragement the least. "Positive role models in my field who were not related to me" were most often reported by home economists (19 responses). One home economist writes, "She is a woman of great human ability and creative talent. She was a terrific teacher and wonderful person. She had a family, home and career. She is now the director of home economics in the public schools." Homemakers (10 responses) also referred to "positive role models" whom they wanted to emulate as positively influencing them and nontraditional (doctors = 5 responses, lawyers = 4 responses) women credited these role models the least. Homemakers (3 references) were the only subjects to state they feel they lacked positive role models and considered this negative in terms of their career development.

"Societal issues" such as "the climate of the 60's, the Great Depression, the Women's Movement, and the need for women doctors in India" were expressed in the open-ended section as positive influencers most often by the nontraditional women (17 responses). The two other groups reported "societal issues" about equally (at most 7 responses per category). "Nonsupportive societal issues" such as "discrimination against women, a limited job market, and victim of the times—no childcare available" were most often cited by homemakers (9 references); lawyers (2 references) reported these issues least often.

Summary

Overall the data indicates that there are significant differences in the employment background of these five groups of women; and, that there are more differences when the five groups representing specific professions are compared than when the sample is analyzed in terms of traditional, nontraditional or homemaker categories. Expectation 1, i.e., that nontraditional career women are more likely to have experienced a large number and wide variety of previous job experiences, receives mixed support. The data suggests that all professionals held more jobs after high school than homemakers and home economists held the largest number of jobs. Homemakers' jobs, however, were in more fields than those of the nontraditionals who followed, and traditional women's after high school jobs represented the least variety of fields. In high school, lawyers had the largest number of jobs, home economists the smallest number. Most often, it was the traditional women who commented that their previous jobs positively influenced their career development; nontraditional women suggested this least often. Nurses reported "characteristics of the job" as positively influencing their career choice most often of the groups. Doctors stated that they "had always wanted to be" in this profession more than the other women. Doctors and home economists were employed in their present positions the longest, nurses the least.

Two reasons for leaving the job—moving and a more desirable position— were cited by the traditional women most often. Nurses also reported "dissatisfaction with the job" as a reason for leaving more than the other groups. Two reasons for leaving—marriage and pregnancy—were reported most often by the homemakers. There were no reasons which doctors or lawyers reported more than the other groups. Nontraditional women together, however, reported least often that they had experienced previous negative job experiences or left a job because of "moving." Homemakers were influenced more than the other groups by their participation in volunteer groups. Expectation 2, i.e., that those women who have experienced a women's (support) group will perceive this experience as having positively influenced their career development, receives some support since lawyers were influenced by their participation in political support groups the most of all the groups. Homemakers also stated that volunteer participation in all women's groups, particularly the League of Women Voters, had encouraged them to take on leadership roles and consider the possibility of part-time employment.

Traditional women most often reported having experienced encouragement from an employment related non-relative. Nontraditional women recalled proportionally the smallest number of employment-related positive role models. Societal issues, on the other hand, influenced nontraditional women more than the others.

Education Variables

The variables included here are the subject's degree, how old she was when she received it; how many years ago that was; the time it took to earn her degree; if she ever discontinued her education and if so, for how long and why; grades in high school, college and post-college; college major; how she financed her education; organizations and leadership positions in high school, college, post-college and presently; and the open-ended responses elicited such as "previous interests, classes or group work, positive and negative role models, books and t.v."

Tables 9 and 10 present the results of F tests from MANOVAs on five professional groups by questionnaire and face-to-face interview responses on 11 education variables (high school, college and post-college grades, organizations and leadership positions in high school, college, post-college and presently). As shown in Tables 9 and 10, there was an overall significant difference, $p < .001$, among the five groups in terms of these variables. MANOVA also showed that nontraditional women are significantly different from the traditional women, $F(11,232) = 16.72, p < .001$. The MANOVA contrasting the five groups in terms of the questionnaire and interview responses also resulted in a significant finding, $p < .033$.

Thirty-nine of the 65 (60%) home economists had advanced degrees (19 (29%) had Ph.D.'s, 20 (31%) had masters); seven of the 59 nurses (12%) had masters and 13 of the 81 homemakers (16%) had advanced degrees (12 had masters, one had a Ph.D.).

Table 9. Results of F Tests from MANOVAs on Five Professional
Groups by Questionnaire and Face-to-Face Interview Responses on
Eleven Educational Variables

Source	Variable	DFHYP/DFERR	MSHYP/MSERR	F
Group		44/889		7.24***
(Home Econ-	High School Grades	4/242	14.347/2.741	5.23***
omists,	College Grades	4/242	10.490/1.985	5.29***
Doctors,	Post-College Grades	4/242	250.279/8.134	30.77***
Lawyers,	No. Organizations in	4/242	3.144/2.463	1.28
Homemakers,	High School			
Nurses)	No. Leadership posi-	4/242	4.806/1.688	2.85*
	tions in High School			
	No. Organizations in	4/242	10.979/2.576	4.26**
	College			
	No. Leadership Posi-	4/242	3.831/1.805	2.12
	tions in College			
	No. Organizations in	4/242	528.228/7.351	71.86***
	Post-College			
	No. Leadership posi-	4/242	611.967/8.863	69.05***
	tions in Post-College			
	No. Organizations	4/242	12.828/2.939	4.36**
	Presently			
	No. Leadership posi-	4/242	2.974/2.434	1.22
	tions presently			
Response		11/232		1.97*
(Question-	High School Grades	1/242	36.019/2.741	13.14***
naire,	College Grades	1/242	1.657/1.985	.84
Interview)	Post-College Grades	1/242	37.275/8.134	4.58*
	No. Organizations in	1/242	13.425/2.436	5.45*
	High School			
	No. Leadership posi-	1/242	.360/1.688	.21
	tions in high school			
	No. Organizations in	1/242	8.248/2.576	3.20
	College			
	No. Leadership posi-	1/242	.246/1.805	.14
	tions in College			
	No. Organizations in	1/242	10.344/7.351	1.41
	Post-College			
	No. Leadership posi-	1/242	13.348/8.863	1.51
	tions in post-college			
	No. Organizations	1/242	.682/2.939	.23
	presently			
	No. Leadership Posi-	1/242	.078/2.434	.03
	tions presently			
Group X		44/889		.81
Response				
Interaction				

*$p < .05$
**$p < .01$
***$p < .001$

Table 10. Means and Standard Deviations of Eleven Education
Variables by Five Professional Groups

Education Variables		Home Economists	Doctors	Lawyers	Home-makers	Nurses
High School Grades[a]	M	2.20	1.51	1.54	1.83	2.21
	SD	2.115	1.620	1.524	1.865	1.381
	N	53	51	44	73	56
College Grades[a]	M	2.36	2.09	2.04	2.49	2.54
	SD	1.506	1.133	1.052	3.204	1.066
	N	60	53	47	73	57
Post–College Grades[a]	M	1.84	2.85	2.43	1.39	1.77
	SD	3.50	2.268	1.367	1.658	3.137
	N	37	47	45	18	14
No. Organizations in High School	M	3.01	2.375	2.950	2.99	2.843
	SD	1.570	1.552	1.632	1.66	1.528
	N	59	48	40	69	51
No. Leadership positions in High School	M	1.166	1.020	1.461	1.41	.725
	SD	1.107	1.344	1.570	1.44	.850
	N	60	48	39	69	51
No. Organizations in College	M	2.466	1.666	2.350	2.20	1.294
	SD	1.567	1.357	1.528	1.96	1.269
	N	60	48	40	70	51
No. Leadership positions in College	M	1.066	.645	1.051	.96	.450
	SD	1.233	1.081	1.168	1.74	.944
	N	60	48	39	70	51
No. Organizations in Post–College	M	4.516	.750	1.550	1.10	.50
	SD	3.614	.862	1.338	3.16	.956
	N	37	48	40	13	18
No. Leadership positions in Post–College	M	3.633	.291	.666	.54	.02
	SD	4.112	.581	.982	3.33	3.305
	N	37	48	39	13	18
No. Organizations Presently	M	3.283	3.083	2.550	2.97	2.096
	SD	1.851	1.748	1.551	1.72	1.694
	N	60	48	40	70	52
No. Leadership Positions Presently	M	1.166	.875	1.528	1.11	.634
	SD	1.786	1.467	.923	1.41	1.414
	N	60	48	39	70	52

Note.   a = (1 = A, 2 = A/B, 3 = B, 4 = B/C, 5 = C, 6 = D)

The questions relating to the degree—age received the degree, how many years ago was that and how many years did it take—were unfortunately asked in a way which is not meaningful in terms of the data analysis because the responses obtained refer to different degrees. For example, one woman responding to "How long did it take you to earn this degree?" responded with the time it took her to earn her Ph.D. after having received her masters, another woman's response included all post-college time and yet another woman's response included all of her post-high school education. In terms of the modal responses, however, all the groups except the lawyers reported four years; lawyers wrote in three years. The modal response in terms of age receiving the degree were 22 for the homemakers and traditional women and 25 for the nontraditional women. The oldest women to earn their degrees were in home economics, more home economists (23%) than the other women (the other groups were 4% or less frequently) earned their degrees in the age ranges of 33–37 years and the oldest degree earner was a 56 year old home economist. This makes sense in terms of the above data showing that more of these women continued their education to earn Ph.D.'s.

Table 11 shows that a chi square comparing the five groups in terms of discontinuing their education before completing their degree resulted in a significant difference, $p < .0001$. An average of 41% of the women discontinued their education. Home economists had discontinued their education most frequently (63%), followed by lawyers, doctors, homemakers and nurses least often (22%). When this same variable was analyzed in terms of the three career categories, no significant difference was found. Again, this information makes sense when one considers that the nontraditional women and the home economists were most likely to continue their formal education beyond the bachelor's degree. Home economists, as a group, however, had less education than doctors or lawyers, yet they interrupted their education more. The information discussing the number of years the woman had discontinued her education is not adequate to be systematically analyzed because the numbers are too scattered to allow for chi square analysis. However, the modal response for the nontraditional women and homemakers was one year and the traditional women three years.

These women offered many reasons why they had quit school; of the 13 reasons generated and which were analyzed (listed in Appendix D), only one of these reasons "employment" as shown in Table 12 significantly differentiated the women, five-group, $p < .022$, three-category, $X^2(2) = 10.73, p < .005$. A total of 40% of the women reported leaving school for employment; of this total, traditional career women cited this reason most often (53%) with homemakers and nontraditionals claiming "employment" much less often (29% or less frequently).

Data from Tables 9 and 10 indicated that an ANOVA showed that nontraditional women received significantly higher high school grades,

Table 11.   Subjects Reporting Having Discontinued Their
Education by Five Professional Groups

	Percent		
	No	Yes	Total N
Home Economists	37	63	65
Doctors	65	35	57
Lawyers	47	53	47
Homemakers	66	34	79
Nurses	78	22	59
Total	59	41	307

Note. $X^2(4) = 27.09$, $p < .0001$

Table 12.   Subjects Reporting Leaving School for Employment

	Percent		
	No	Yes	Total N
Home Economists	41	59	41
Doctors	71	29	17
Lawyers	76	24	25
Homemakers	73	27	26
Nurses	53	47	15
Total	60	40	124

Note. $X^2(4) = 11.47$, $p < .022$

$F(1,242) = 13.76$, $p < .001$, and higher college grades, $F(1,242) = 17.95$, $p < .001$, than the traditional women. Earning excellent grades seemed to effect these nontraditional women as one lawyer stated, "Having been a bright student it was taken for granted by high school teachers that I would go on to college and 'become something'." Data from Tables 9 and 10 also indicate that ANOVA shows that questionnaire responders reported significantly higher high school grades, $F(1,242) = 13.14$, $p < .001$, than the interview subjects. Although the chi square data was not sufficient for statistical analysis, the frequencies supported this finding by showing that doctors and lawyers consistently received the higher grades in high school (59% received A averages) and college (27% received A averages), homemakers followed and then traditional women (26% received A averages in high school; 8% received A averages in college). Of the women who did receive grades during their post-college education, homemakers received the highest ones (67% received A averages) followed by nurses, home economists, doctors and lawyers (18% received A averages). Tables 9 and 10 show that, again, the ANOVA contrast demonstrates that the questionnaire responders reported significantly higher grades during their post-college education than the face-to-face interviewees, $F(1,242) = 4.59$, $p < .033$.

The question about college major generated a large number of responses; of the 15 college majors written in and coded (complete list in Appendix D), four had data sufficient to analyze which also resulted in significant differences for the five groups. Table 32 (in Appendix G) presents the results discussing these four majors. "Science" was chosen most often by the doctors (87%) and least often by the lawyers (2%), $p < .0001$. As could be expected, "home economics" was chosen most often by the home economists (79%) in the five-way analysis, $p < .0001$; nurses and doctors never chose home economics as a college major. Also as expected, the nurses (95%) chose "nursing" the most, $p < .0001$, and nontraditional women (1%) chose "nursing" least often in the five-profession, $p < .0001$ and three-career, $X^2(2) = 80.11$, $p < .0001$, analyses. Although there was not sufficient data to perform a chi square analysis, lawyers chose "political science" most often and homemakers chose "education" most often.

These women managed to finance their education from many sources. Table 13 shows that four of the eight methods coded resulted in significant differences (complete list in Appendix D). "Parents" support was significantly different, $p < .039$, when contrasting the five groups but not the three career categories. The majority of all women (66%) reported parental support. Homemakers used financial support from their parents most often (75%), and home economists least often (54%). A majority of the women (56%) also financed some of their education by working. Home economists worked to support their education the most (71%), lawyers used this source next, then doctors, homemakers, and nurses (47%).

Analysis of "scholarships and fellowships" as a source of college/post-college financial aid by the five groups resulted in a trend difference, $p < .097$, with nurses (40%) using this source first, doctors second, lawyers third, home economists fourth and homemakers fifth (19%). Sixteen percent of the women used "loans and borrowed" to support part of their education. Lawyers (30%) took "loans from institutions and borrowed from friends" significantly more, $p < .002$, than the other four groups with homemakers (5%) using loans the least often. When given the chance to freely discuss events which positively

Table 13. Sources of Financing One's Education by Five Professional Groups

Financial Source	Home Economists Percent No	Yes	N	Doctors Percent No	Yes	N	Lawyers Percent No	Yes	N	Homemakers Percent No	Yes	N	Nurses Percent No	Yes	N	Total Percent No	Yes	N
Parents $X^2(4) = 10.10$, $p < .039$	46%	54%	65	42%	58%	55	28%	72%	47	29%	75%	76	29%	71%	59	34%	66%	302
Working $X^2(4) = 9.69$, $p < .046$	29%	71%	65	47%	53%	55	40%	60%	47	51%	49%	77	53%	47%	58	44%	56%	302
Scholarships or Fellowships $X^2(4) = 7.87$, $p < .097$	71%	29%	65	64%	36%	55	66%	34%	47	81%	19%	77	60%	40%	58	69%	31%	302
Loans $X^2(4) = 17.50$, $p < .002$	89%	11%	65	82%	18%	55	70%	30%	47	95%	5%	77	76%	24%	58	84%	16%	302

supported their career development, home economists (11 references) reported using financial resources for their higher education far more often than any of the other groups. For the most part, it was the home economics women pursuing Ph.D.'s who had secured assistantships and offered this response. Homemakers never gave "financial support" as a source of encouragement. Homemakers (4 references), on the other hand, said their "financial situation" hindered their career development more than the other groups and nontraditional women never reported finances as limiting their career plans. One lawyer clearly stated the importance of money throughout one's career development, "Money, lack thereof, is a critical factor for acquiring sufficient education. Money will solve most problems (basic tuition and living costs, child care, domestic help). Money will also determine the type of education— enough for a professional degree? Enough for a good school rather than Podunk U? With benefits in later life of better contacts, enough to really get the most out of the entire experience, enough to dress well when you finally interview and are on the job, enough so you don't have to stint on doing things with kids when you have limited time with them."

Another aspect of the school experience which does not relate to the subject's major or financial situation, concerns participation in organizations and leadership positions held. Figure 2 shows that the three category analysis yielded significant differences, $X^2(10) = 20.48$, $p < .025$, with homemakers (modal response = at least 5, mean = 3.0) being involved in the largest number of organizations in high school and nontraditional women (modal response = 2, mean = 2.7) the least. Data from Tables 9 and 10 show that ANOVA suggest that the interviewees reported significantly more involvement in high school organizations than the women responding to the questionnaire, $F(1,242) = 5.45$, $p < .020$. Unfortunately, the responses were too scattered to be systematically analyzed by the five groups. The rest of the variables concerned with organization and leadership behaviors throughout high school and at the time the study was conducted resulted in no significant differences.

When given the opportunity to respond to the open-ended questions dealing with experiences related to the woman's career development, a number of other education-related ideas were suggested. "Previous interests and classes" were positive influencers especially for home economists (31 references) who frequently commented about their 4-H activities. Homemakers (17 references) followed with the remaining three groups being about equal (8 references or less per group) in recalling "previous interests." Although almost no difference was noted between the five groups, "previous group work" such as assertiveness training and life-career planning workshops was most often suggested as supportive of a career decision by homemakers (3 references). "College memories" elicited some very positive and influential memories for some nurses and lawyers and negative remembrances for some homemakers, doctors and home economists. One nursing subject recalls

Figure 2:   Number of Organizations in High School by Three
             Career Categories.
             Total N = 267, $p < .025$

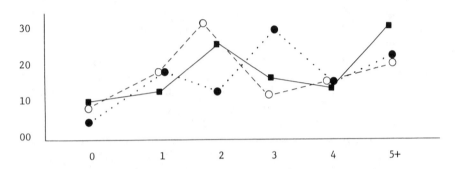

O-- Nontraditionals (N=88)
●··· Traditionals (N=110)
■— Homemakers (N=69)

"Living with three other nursing students—all with above average grade point averages—during my three years in nursing school at the medical center—a *very close, supportive healthy relationship*—for three years which continues today." Three nurses and two lawyers stated that they had gone to all women's colleges where it was expected that women would not only contribute to society, but would also be supportive of other women. "At the women's college—in an atmosphere where women were *expected* to pursue their interests, be it career or otherwise, and where women were *encouraged* to enter fields traditionally reserved for men, the growth of a strong career decision flourished. There was a strength in numbers of other women, if you will, and never a sense of 'The men do that—you go find a nice husband." In direct contrast to their positive experiences, three homemakers, two doctors and two home economists recalled environments which were more conducive to socializing than studying. Three nurses and two lawyers also recalled specific books, "Hokey as it may sound, I fell in love with The U.S. Constitution. I wanted to be a lawyer so as to help preserve it." None of the homemakers, home economists or doctors alluded to these sources.

"Non-related significant others contacted in the educational environment" were also reported as both positive and negative influences. In terms of role models whom the subjects emulated, only three doctors and one lawyer recalled any. Home economists did, however, credit a large number of school people (22 references) with having encouraged them with their career aspirations. "The Dean told me I should get my Ph.D. degree. I had never

considered it before but respected the suggestion and studied for the Ph.D."
Doctors followed (18 references), then came homemakers (17 references),
lawyers (8 references), and nurses (3 references). Nurses (3 references)
remembered the largest number of people from school who discouraged them
from their career plans; doctors, lawyers, and homemakers again fell in the
middle and home economists never mentioned any discouraging school people.
One homemaker's response exemplifies the discouragement she experienced as
an adolescent. "The chairman of Mechanical Engineering at the university
advised me to 'do something feminine' when I wrote him as a 9th grader asking
about high school preparation courses for engineering."

Summary

Similar to the findings in the employment section, more five group, (doctor,
lawyer, home economist, nurse and homemaker) than three category,
(nontraditional, traditional and homemaker) analyses resulted in significant
differences. Doctors and lawyers had the most advanced degrees, nurses the
least. Home economists were the oldest when they earned these higher degrees
and were the group which discontinued their education most. The only reason
for leaving school which differentiated the three categories of women was
"employment." Traditional women reported employment most often and
nontraditional and homemaker women claimed employment much less often.

Nontraditional women earned the highest grades in high school and
college. College majors most often reported were science for doctors, political
science for lawyers, nursing for nurses, home economics for home economists
and education for homemakers. Several sources of financial support resulted in
significant differences among the women. Although the majority of all women
reported "parents" and "working" as sources of financial support, homemakers
claimed "parents" most and home economists claimed "working" most. Nurses
utilized "scholarships and fellowships" most of the groups and lawyers
reported "loans and borrowing" more than the others. Homemakers cited
finances as having presented problems with their career plans; nontraditional
women never mentioned financial problems interfering with their career plans.
In high school, homemakers participated in the most organizations,
nontraditionals the least. Homemakers also experienced the most and were
most often positively influenced by their group experiences. Home economists
were the women most influenced by "previous interests and classes." "College
memories" were recalled as more positive for the nurses and lawyers and more
negative for the homemakers, home economists and doctors. Expectation 3,
i.e., that more pioneer career women will have received positive support from a
professor or other influential role model during their college and post-college
training, was supported; only doctors and lawyers, in fact mentioned positive
school-related role models influencing their career plans. Home economists

credited the largest number of school-related people with having encouraged their career aspirations.

Childhood Family Background Variables

The variables which assess family background include the subject's race, her parents' age in terms of how long they were alive during the subject's lifetime, her parents' marital status, parents' occupation before she was five, five-18 years, and 18 years and older, parents educational background, her family constellation (number of children in her family, birth order, sex of siblings), if anyone lived with her family during her childhood and if so, their relationship to the subject, religious background, and how she perceived her relationship with her parents. Other open-ended responses relating to family background included positive and negative role models, encouragement and discouragement from relatives, and the presence of "sick" relatives were suggested.

Data from Tables 14 and 15 show that a three category MANOVA indicated that the nontraditional women are significantly different, $F(7,283) =$

Table 14. Results of F Tests from MANOVAs on Five Professional Groups by Questionnaire, Phone Interview and Face-to-Face Interview Responses on Seven Family Variables

Source	Variable	DFHYP/DFERR	MSHYP/MSERR	F
Group		28/1021		
(Home Econ-	Mother's Age	4/289	.452/ .523	1.38
omist,	Father's Age	4/289	.444/ .695	.64
Doctors,	Mother's Education	4/289	4.562/2.487	1.83
Lawyers,	Father's Education	4/289	21.090/5.695	3.70*
Homemakers,	No. Children in Subject's	4/289	4.516/3.035	1.49
Nurses)	Family			
	Subject's Birth Order	4/289	2.287/2.330	.98
	No. Male Siblings	4/289	1.469/1.768	.83
Response		14/566		1.32
(Question-				
naire, Mini-				
Phone Inter-				
view, Face-				
to-Face				
Interview)				
Group X		56/1529		1.04
Response				
Interaction				

*p < .001

Table 15.   Means and Standard Deviations of Seven Family Variables By
Five Professional Groups

Family Variable		Home Economists	Doctors	Lawyers	Home-makers	Nurses
Mother's Age	M	5.892	5.701	5.829	5.888	5.915
1=died or left when	SD	.664	1.051	.816	.612	.384
subject was 0-2 yr	N	65	57	47	81	59
2=...subject was 3-5						
3=...subject was 6-10						
4=...subject was 11-15						
5=...subject was 21+						
Father's Age	M	5.815	5.824	5.787	5.888	5.661
1=died or left when	SD	.899	.684	.858	.524	1.138
subject was 0-2 yr	N	65	57	47	81	59
2=...subject was 3-5						
3=...subject was 6-10						
4=...subject was 11-15						
5=...subject was 21+						
Mother's Education	M	2.369	2.982	3.065	2.835	2.949
1=less than high	SD	1.281	1.977	1.569	1.505	1.431
school	N	65	57	46	79	59
7=Ph.D., M.D., J.D.						
Father's Education	M	2.476	3.982	3.586	3.437	3.000
1=less than high	SD	1.896	2.850	2.663	2.438	1.956
school	N	65	57	46	80	59
7=Ph.D., M.D., J.D.						
# Children in Sub-	M	3.328	3.517	2.893	3.308	3.711
ject's Family	SD	1.869	1.925	1.005	1.927	1.682
1=only child	N	64	56	47	81	59
Subject's Birth Order	M	2.061	2.107	1.914	2.395	2.305
1=1st born	SD	1.647	1.274	.951	1.779	1.511
	N	65	56	47	81	59
# of Male Siblings	M	1.234	1.303	1.042	1.333	1.525
0=None	SD	1.353	1.249	.858	1.612	1.222
	N	64	56	47	81	59

2.37, $p < .023$, from traditional women with respect to the seven family
background variables analyzed (mother's age, father's age, mother's education,
father's education, number of children in her family, her birth order, and
number of male siblings she had). The overall MANOVA only suggested a
trend difference, $p < .092$, for all five of the groups of women in terms of these
variables.

Most of the women were "caucasian" with most non-whites foreignborn doctors (e.g., Indians). The data discussing mother's and father's age in terms of their presence in the subject's life also fell primarily into one category— "lived together throughout the subject's life"—and resulted in no significant differences. Examination of the results, however, shows that doctors and lawyers are somewhat different from the other groups in that 5% of lawyers were the only subjects who had mothers who died before they were five years old; other groups fell into this category at most 1% of the time. The traditional women, on the other hand, were the only subjects (6%) who had fathers who died in their early youths.

Analyses of parents' occupations resulted in a few significant differences. Results suggest that nontraditional women were reared by the most nontraditional mothers and this definitely seems to have had a very positive effect on the subjects' career development as will be illustrated in the open-ended responses. Before the age of five, mother's occupation does not provide adequate data to be statistically analyzed, though there is a trend suggesting that doctors and nurses had the most mothers who were professionals and homemakers had the most mothers who were homemakers (complete list of mother's occupation is in Appendix D). Table 16 shows that this data analyzed in terms of whether the mother was in the same field as her daughter and for the ages 5–18 years and 18 years and older simply shows that doctors' mothers were most likely to be in nontraditional careers, nurses' mothers least likely to be homemakers. Table 33 (in Appendix G) shows that few mothers were in the same field except, as one might expect, homemakers' mothers, who were most likely to be homemakers.

Table 16.   Mother's Occupation When the Subject was 5–18 Years Old by Five Professional Groups

| | Percent | | | |
	Homemaker	Professional	Nonprofessional Other	Total N
Home Economists	66	9	25	64
Doctors	63	21	15	52
Lawyers	62	2	36	47
Homemakers	69	8	23	80
Nurses	47	22	30	59
Total	62	13	25	302

Note. $X^2(8) = 20.58$, $p < .008$

From the open-ended section, "positive family role models" (usually cited as the subject's mother) whom the subject desired to be like was cited most often by doctors (17 references) followed by homemakers (14 references) then nurses (11 references) and home economists (11 responses) and lawyers (6 responses). Illustrative of the doctors' lengthy and enthusiastic comments about their mothers, one subject wrote "My original decision to become an M.D. was made at about 10 years. Undoubtedly the tremendous respect of others and the competence of my mother were responsible for my decision. She was greatly loved and respected in the community. Everyone felt that she was contributing to the community so much that no one asked her (in my presence anyway) why she was working. Certainly the fact that my mother was very successfully a doctor, a mother and a wife, I felt that there would be no significant problems to doing it myself." On the other hand, "negative family role models" (most often the subject's mother) whom the subject did not want to copy were most often reported by homemakers (7 references) and lawyers (6 references). One lawyer recalls "My mother was a nag and an unhappy person when a housewife, she became more relaxed at home and happy after employment." Doctors, home economists and nurses reported "negative familial role models" less and about equally (3 references or less/group).

In terms of father's occupation, the data suggests that the nontraditional women (43%), particularly the doctors (49%) had by far the largest proportion of professional fathers (complete list of father's occupation in Appendix D). Although the data was analyzed in terms of each of the three age ranges, the data will be reported only once since father's occupation resulted in similar findings regardless of the subject's age. Table 17 shows that significant differences were found for both the five group, $p < .002$ and three category, $X^2(6) = 13.53$, $p < .035$, comparisons. Doctors (49%) and lawyers (36%) most often had professional fathers, home economists (36%) had farming fathers and nurses (43%) and homemakers (35%) had fathers in many "other" jobs (ranging from salesworker to craftsperson). The analysis of the same field as daughter was somewhat meaningless since not many fathers would be nurses, home economists or homemakers. Thus, the finding that doctors and lawyers (10%) had more fathers in their same career field than the other groups (5% or less frequently) or more specifically that doctors and lawyers (10%) were the only subjects to have fathers in their same occupation, is no surprise.

Data from Tables 14 and 15 show that mother's education was not significantly different for the three groups. Only trend differences of an ANOVA, $F(1,289) = 3.22$, $p < .074$, indicated that nontraditional women's mothers' had higher educational backgrounds than traditional mothers. Chi square results were also nonsignificant. The modal response for all groups, except doctors, was high school degree; the modal responses for doctors' mothers were less than high school and college. Nontraditional women (13%), however, had the most mothers with professional degrees. The homemakers

Table 17.   Father's Occupation When the Subject Was Younger than 5
Years Old by Five Professional Groups

| | Percent | | | | |
	Professional	Manager/ Administrator	Farmer/ Farm Mgr.	Other	Total N
Home Economists	28	5	36	31	61
Doctors	49	9	13	29	55
Lawyers	36	23	6	34	47
Homemakers	31	15	19	35	80
Nurses	34	11	13	43	56
Total	35	12	18	34	299

Note. $X^2(12) = 30.91$, $\underline{p} < .002$

followed, then the traditional women (1%). Data from Tables 14 and 15 show
that an ANOVA of father's education was significant, $F(1,289) = 11.85, p <$
.001, with nontraditional women's fathers receiving more higher degrees than
the traditional women's fathers. Table 18 shows that chi square analysis of
father's education resulted in trend differences for the five groups, $p < .066$, and
three categories, $X^2(8) = 13.96$, $p < .083$, which support the ANOVA finding.
The notable findings are that the traditional women had the fewest fathers who
were professionals and home economists' fathers had the least education of all
the groups.

The family constellation variables including number of siblings, birth
order and sex of siblings did not result in significant differences. In the open-
ended section, however, doctors (3 references), home economists (3 references)
and homemakers (3 references) all made references to their family constellation
as having been supportive of their career development. For example, one
doctor commented that she felt her position, the youngest of three daughters,
resulted in her receiving the expectations and hopes from her father that would
have gone to a son. A home economist states "Only sharing at home
responsibilities as a child taught me I didn't want to spend my life as a
'homemaker.' With so many older brothers it was easy to observe that
excitement wasn't found at home." The lawyers and nurses (1 response)
reported "family constellation" issues less often.

Table 19 shows that chi square analysis of the subject's religious
background resulted in significant differences for both the five, $p < .0001$, and
three group, $X^2(4) = 29.53$, $p < .0001$, analyses. As expected from general

Table 18. Father's Education by Five Professional Groups

	Less Than High School	High School	Some College	College Degree	Prof. Degree	Total N
		Percent				
Home Economists	37	32	12	6	12	65
Doctors	19	26	11	14	30	57
Lawyers	16	23	25	14	23	44
Homemakers	18	21	20	17	24	76
Nurses	24	27	15	20	14	59
Total	23	26	16	14	20	301

Note. $X^2(16) = 25.20$, $p < .066$

Table 19. Religious Background by Five Professional Groups

	Jewish, Unitarian, Other	Catholic	Protestant	Total N
	Percent			
Home Economists	5	9	86	65
Doctors	13	22	65	55
Lawyers	30	28	41	46
Homemakers	2	21	77	81
Nurses	3	25	71	59
Total	9	21	70	306

Note. $X^2(8) = 45.67$, $p < .0001$

population statistics, the modal response for all groups was Protestant. Besides this, the most salient finding is that compared to the other groups, lawyers were most Jewish (30%) and least Protestant (41%). Home economists were most Protestant (86%). Except for home economists (who were 9% Catholic), Catholics represented from 21% to 28% of all groups. In the open-ended section discussing experiences which positively influenced career development, doctors (5 references) cited religious-related experiences the most; the other groups rarely referred to influential religious experiences (1 reference/group).

Doctors (6 references) and nurses (5 references) reported that "sickness" of a family member or close significant other positively influenced their career decision much more than the other women (at most 1 response/group).

Homemakers (50 responses) and home economists (48 responses) attributed "encouragement from a relative" for career choice as positive influencers of their career development more than doctors (39 references), lawyers (33 references), or nurses (26 references). A Ph.D. home economist, for example, reported "The significant persons in my life (parents, grandparents, aunts, uncles, *husband* and certain professors) have expected me to work to capacity and to achieve success. I have never been told 'you can't (or shouldn't) do that'—'You're only a girl.'" Homemakers (21 references) also reported "discouragement from a relative" for a career choice much more often than the other groups. Unlike the above mentioned encouragement to be a homemaker, these homemakers' responses referred to the discouragement they experienced considering employment outside of the home. "I wanted to enter nursing but my father decided it was too strenuous a profession for girls, and was prepared to finance a secretarial course. When I was young it was customary to do what your parents decided was best for you—I have always regretted not being a nurse." Or another homemaker writes "It turns out that though my husband thinks and says he would like me to work, when it comes down to sharing responsibilities at home his career commitment is so strong that sacrificing any part of it so that I can have a career too is not possible. I will continue that I have chosen to stay at home, abandoning my plans to become a public health microbiologist, because I am very committed to my marriage and children, and did not feel that having a career was worth breaking up the marriage and family that we had established." The traditionals (4 per group) reported "discouragement" the least often of the groups.

Summary

Family variables also resulted in more differences when comparisons among the five groups as opposed to the three categories were made. About half the family background hypotheses tested resulted in significant differences. The majority of the women were caucasian and were reared by both of their parents. Expectation 4, i.e., that there are significant positive correlations between nontraditional career status and being the daughter of an employed mother, received mixed support. Of all the groups, nurses and doctors had the largest number of employed mothers; lawyers were among the lowest. Homemakers had the most fulltime homemakers for mothers. Doctors most often reported having been positively influenced by a family role model (most often refers to subject's mother) and lawyers the least. Homemakers and lawyers, on the other hand, recalled the most "negative family role models." Expectation 5, i.e., that daughters' nontraditional career performance will be correlated with mothers' nontraditional career performance, receives support. Proportionally, nontraditional women, particularly the doctors, did experience the largest number of nontraditional mothers and mothers with advanced degrees. Homemakers and lawyers recalled the largest number of negative family role models, i.e., employed mothers whom they did not emulate. Nontraditional women, particularly the doctors, had the most fathers who were professionals and who were in their same occupations. The fathers of the doctors and homemakers had earned the highest degrees.

Expectation 6 (that first born status positively correlates with nontraditional career status), Expectation 7 (that being a female without male siblings positively correlates with nontraditional career status) and Expectation 8 (that nontraditional women are more likely to have perceived their childhood relationship with their mother as more hostile than nurturant) were not supported. Doctors, home economists and homemakers did, however, make reference to their family constellation as having positively influenced their career development. Expectation 9 (Jewish and Unitarian parents) received mixed support. The lawyers came from the largest number of Jewish families. They also, however, had proportionately the largest number of Catholic parents. Doctors cited religious-related experiences as having positively influenced their career decisions most often of the groups. Homemakers reported the most encouragement from relatives to continue with their career plans—homemaking—and the most discouragement from relatives when considering employment outside the home. Doctors and nurses most often recalled "sickness" of a family member or close significant other as having positively influenced their career decision.

Environmental Variables

Environmental variables tested encompass the women's interests, social and marital situations. Specifically, the variables analyzed included the woman's childhood and present hobbies, the age of her first date, marital and career status, the number of children she has, her oldest and youngest children's ages, and how old she was when she first became a mother, her living arrangement if she was single, her commitment to her present marital and career situation, and close supportive relationships both during her higher education days and presently.

Tables 20 and 21 present the results of F tests from MANOVAs on five professional groups by questionnaire, phone-interview and face-to-face interview responses on five self/environment variables (number of children subject has, commitment to present marital/career situation, age, height and weight). Data from Tables 20 and 21 show that all professionals are

Table 20.   Results of F Tests from MANOVAs on Five Professional
Groups By Questionnaire, Phone Interview and Face-to-Face Interview
Responses on Five Self/Environment Variables

Source	Variable	DFHYP/DFERR	MSHYP/MSERR	F
Group		20/916		8.88***
(Home Econ-	No. Children Subject	4/280	48.748/1.714	28.44***
omist,	Has			
Doctors,	Commitment to	4/280	6.330/1.454	4.34**
Lawyers,	Present Marital/			
Homemakers,	Career Situation			
Nurses)	Age	4/280	3418.553/169.341	20.19***
	Height	4/280	19.450/7.092	2.74*
	Weight	4/280	477.470/416.602	1.15
Response		10/552		.55
(Question-				
naire,				
Mini-Phone				
Interview,				
Face-to-				
Face				
Interview)				
Group X		40/1205.851		.85
Response				
Inter-				
action				

*p < .05
**p < .01
***p < .001

significantly different from the homemakers, $F(5,276) = 18.37$, $p < .001$, and
nontraditional career women are significantly different from the traditional
women, $F(5,276) = 7.48$, $p < .001$, in terms of these variables. Chi square
comparison of the women's hobbies as children and presently supports that
there are significant differences between the groups. Although an extremely
long list of hobbies was generated by these women, of the 17 which had
sufficient data to be coded and analyzed by chi square analysis, only a few were
preferred by one group significantly more than the other groups (complete list
in Appendix D). Table 22 shows that as children, only "domestic activities"
(e.g., embroidery, knitting, floral arranging, playing house) significantly
differentiated the five groups, $p < .0001$, and three groups, $X^2(2) = 15.52$, $p <$
.0004. Fifty-seven percent of the home economists but only 10% of the lawyers
reported such childhood activities, with the other groups ranging from 27 to
37%. Frequency tables show that the two childhood hobbies chosen most by

Table 21. Means and Standard Deviations of Five Self/Environment Variables by Five Professional Groups

Environment/ Self Variables		Home Economists	Doctors	Lawyers	Homemakers	Nurses
No. Children Subject Has 0 = None	M SD N	.846 1.175 65	1.824 1.743 57	1.297 1.487 47	2.617 1.199 81	.491 .897 59
Commitment to Present Marital/Career Situation 1 = Weak	M SD N	4.380 1.312 63	4.921 1.246 51	4.422 .839 45	4.227 1.358 79	4.000 1.033 59
Age (Years)	M SD N	41.625 13.381 64	50.964 14.561 57	36.212 11.082 47	45.925 14.738 81	31.372 8.511 59
Height (Inches)	M SD N	65.437 2.695 64	64.263 2.844 57	65.340 2.425 47	64.592 2.696 81	65.372 2.664 59
Weight (Pounds)	M SD N	137.48 23.694 64	134.94 20.112 57	130.978 18.281 46	131.839 20.303 81	131.440 17.465 59

Table 22. Childhood Hobby—Domestic Activities—By Five Professional Groups

	Percent No	Yes	Total N
Home Economists	43	57	56
Doctors	68	32	50
Lawyers	90	10	40
Homemakers	73	27	70
Nurses	63	37	52
Total	66	34	268

Note. $X^2(4) = 25.47$, $p < .0001$

each group were: doctors: sports (54%) and reading (44%); lawyers: sports (68%) and reading (48%); home economists: domestic activities (57%) and sports (52%); nurses: sports (67%) and domestic activities (37%); and homemakers: sports (47%) and reading (41%). Data from Tables 3 and 4 show that the ANOVA comparison of Factor 9, Sex Appropriate Orientation, $F(1,263) = 12.84$, $p < .001$, suggests that the professionals played with girls more and were more feminine than the homemakers as children.

Table 23 shows that several present hobbies resulted in significant chi square differences. "Sports," chosen most often by nurses (71%) followed closely by lawyers, then homemakers, home economists and doctors (43%) was significant in terms of the five group comparison, $p < .024$, but not in terms of the three category comparisons. "Arts and Crafts," chosen 25% of the time by all women, resulted in a trend difference in the five group analysis, $p < .054$, but not the three category analysis. Nurses (35%) chose "Arts and Crafts" the most then came homemakers, doctors, home economists, and lawyers (14%). As adults, interest in "domestic activities" was similar to the childhood results. The five-way, $p < .001$, analysis was significant with the home economists first (64%) and the nontraditionals, particularly the lawyers (17%) last. One doctor and one lawyer cited their interest in "meditation" as positively influencing their careers. Frequency tables show that the first two hobbies chosen most often by each group were the same as the childhood choices for all the groups except the homemakers who changed to sports as most often preferred and domestic activities second.

Another interest, dating, resulted in no significant differences between the groups with respect to the age of the subject's first date. The modal response given was 15 for the traditionals and homemakers and 17 for the nontraditionals.

Table 24 shows that marital status resulted in chi square significant differences for both five, $p < .0001$, and three, $X^2(4) = 51.82$, $p < .0001$, groups analyses. The modal response for all of the groups except nurses was "married" (64%); of those women who were single, the largest number of them were the nurses (46%) and smallest number were homemakers (1%). The homemakers' response is obvious by their classification as "homemaker"; the nurses difference should be considered in light of the age variable discussed in the next section (the nurses are the youngest sample, which could account for fewer of them being married). Figure 3 shows that homemakers (41%) and doctors (45%) have been married the longest amount of time, at least 21 years and nurses (64%) the shortest (5 years or less) by the five way, $X^2(12) = 71.96$, $p < .0001$, chi square analysis.

Data from Tables 20 and 21 indicate that ANOVA analyses show, $F(1,280) = 29.92$, $p < .001$, that nontraditional women have more children than traditional women. Frequency tables, however show that the modal response for homemakers is two children and zero children for all four of the other

Table 23. Present Hobbies by Five Professional Groups

Present Hobby	Home Economists Percent No	Yes	N	Doctors Percent No	Yes	N	Lawyers Percent No	Yes	N	Homemakers Percent No	Yes	N	Nurses Percent No	Yes	N	Total Percent No	Yes	N
Sports $x^2(4) = 11.23$, p .024	54%	46%	56	57%	43%	44	34%	66%	35	47%	53%	68	29%	71%	49	45%	55%	252
Arts and Crafts $x^2(4) = 9.31$, $p < .054$	84%	16%	56	77%	23%	44	86%	14%	36	68%	32%	68	65%	35%	49	75%	25%	253
Domestic Activities $x^2(4) = 23.88$, p .0001	36%	64%	56	66%	34%	44	83%	17%	36	47%	53%	68	55%	45%	49	55%	45%	253

Table 24.   Marital Status by Five Professional Groups

	Single	Married	Percent Divorced, Separated or Widowed	Total N
Home Economists	35	48	17	65
Doctors	12	70	18	57
Lawyers	32	57	11	47
Homemakers	1	91	7	81
Nurses	46	41	14	59
Total	24	64	13	309

Note. $X^2(8) = 59.55$, $p < .0001$

Figure 3:   Number of Years Married by Five Professional
Groups.
(Total $N = 202$, $p < .0001$)

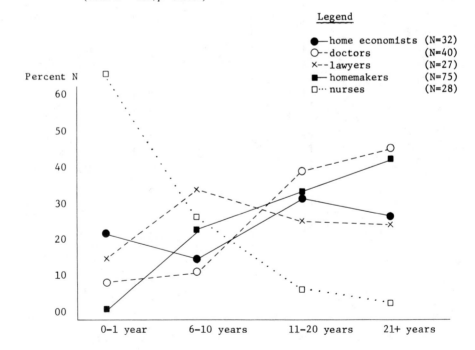

Legend

●—home economists (N=32)
○--doctors   (N=40)
×--lawyers   (N=27)
■—homemakers   (N=75)
□··· nurses   (N=28)

groups. Figure 4 shows that homemakers (39%) were the youngest, 23–25 years old, when they gave birth to their first child; doctors (42%) were the oldest when they gave birth to their first child at age 30–39 as demonstrated in the five way, $X^2(12) = 27.37, p < .007$, chi square. Figure 5 demonstrates that in conjunction with this finding is the five group, $X^2(12) = 30.84, p < .002$, chi square analysis showing that homemakers (39%) are mothers of the oldest children, at least 22 years old, and nurses (61%) the youngest children, 6 years or younger.

Unfortunately, the question concerning "Which marital/career situation best fits you?" was not asked in a way which could be readily analyzed. Because of this, the modal response for each group will be reported. Doctors, lawyers and home economists all chose #14, "I am combining marriage and childrearing with employment" from the married with children category most often. Nurses most frequently chose #10, "I anticipate remaining employed before children are born, then resuming employment after my youngest child is _____" from the married without children category. Homemakers supported the criteria of selection used in this research by choosing #12, "I am a full-time homemaker and anticipate remaining a full-time homemaker" from the married with children category.

Data from Tables 20 and 21 show that an ANOVA comparison of the subject's commitment to this choice resulted in nontraditional women being significantly more committed to their present situation than the traditional women, $F(1,280) = 8.35, p < .004$. The modal response for all groups was, however, 5 "very strong" on a five-point scale. Of the open-ended responses which relate to this issue, homemakers (8 responses) reported more "regrets" with their present lives. Several of these homemakers, in fact, wrote about the anger and resentment they are experiencing because they feel trapped at home with their children and cannot afford the time or money to pursue a career. "With two small children and only an average financial situation, I am at present, unable to pursue a new career goal—specifically, an M.S. in guidance. I wish now that I had pushed to finish my masters immediately after college as I somewhat resent and regret that all my efforts were oriented towards furthering my husband professionally. We are happily married, have two lovely children and a beautiful home/environment but I'm bored and unchallenged with housekeeping etc. However, full time employment would not help my organization or my present family duties. Less than full time employment is not financially practical as I am only trained to teach." Four nontraditional professional women also expressed dissatisfaction with their present marital/career situations. One doctor, regretting that she has no social life, suggested to all professional women that they carefully balance their careers and social lives. One lawyer complained that she does not have any women colleagues to start a law firm with and may eventually leave law if the situation does not change. Three nurses were sorry they ended up nurses rather than doctors or scientists; these women felt that inadequate guidance led them to

Figure 4: Subject's Age at Birth of First Child by Five
Professional Groups.
(Total N = 183, $p < .007$)

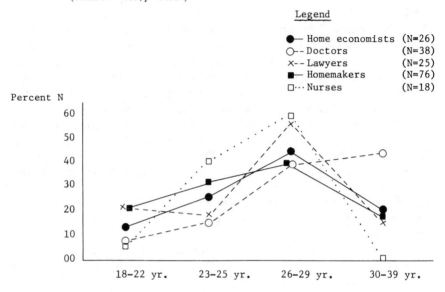

Figure 5: Oldest Child's Age by Five Professional Groups.
(Total N = 184, $p < .002$)

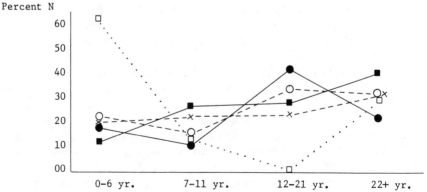

believe that the only career options open to them had been nursing or teaching. "Father made most decisions for *me* including school and ultimately career . . . I frequently do day dream of being a marine biologist or would trade places to be a zoologist any day but have instead decided to channel energy to make nursing more professionally recognized and respected." No home economists reported "regrets" with their present lives.

When discussing events which influenced their career development in the open-ended portion of the questionnaire, homemakers (57 references) far more than any of the other groups reported that "family obligations," as noted earlier, kept them out of careers. Nurses (11 references) reported "family obligations" second and the other three groups less often and about equally (6 references/group). "Family obligations" were also cited as positive influencers of some women's careers. Ten home economists offered this possibility the most followed by doctors and nurses, lawyers and homemakers (2 references). One home economist put it well. "Initial mind set of 'putting husband through' graduate school postponed the traditional mother/housewife role. This allowed time/opportunity to realize personal commitment to professional career."

Did these women think about their future marital/career plans when they were in high school and college? Data from Tables 3 and 4 show that ANOVA comparisons suggest with a trend difference, $F(1,263) = 3.76$, $p < .054$, that homemakers had a "positive orientation towards marriage and children" (Factor 2) more than the professionals; in contrast, the professionals were significantly, $F(1,263) = 8.46$, $p < .004$, more "oriented towards nontraditional careers" (Factor 4) than the homemakers. ANOVA analysis supports that nontraditional women were significantly more, $F(1,263) = 210.44$, $p < .001$, nontraditionally career oriented than the traditionals. Table 25 shows that regression equations also support this finding; 43% of the variance of Factor 4—Nontraditional career orientation—is explained by doctors (25%) and lawyers (17%), $p < .0001$. One doctor describes this longterm commitment, "As I went through childhood my parents' disagreements helped me in a positive way, i.e. I always wanted to have a career which would make me self-sufficient and financially independent, whether I got married or not."

Questions concerning past supportive relationships resulted in no significant differences. Examination of the frequency data shows, however, that of the single women responding to the questions, lawyers were the only group to have more men than women friends in college and post-college years. Homemakers (28%) had proportionally the most women friends of all the groups during college and nurses (57%) had the most women friends during post-college years. Chi square analysis of "the people who are presently closest to me" resulted in significant differences between the groups. Table 26 shows that the majority of all women sampled (75%) chose men more than women as their closest friend. Five group analysis, $p < .0015$, and three category analysis,

Table 25.   Background Variables Which Predict
"Nontraditional Career Orientation" (Factor 4)
(Factor 4 — Positive Variables: High School Career
Orientation was Nontraditional, College
Career Orientation was Nontraditional
— Negative Variables: High School Career
Orientation was Traditional, College
Career Orientation was Traditional)

Source	Beta	F Value	Probability
Doctors	+	156.76	.0001
Lawyers	+	83.19	.0001

Note.   Nontraditional career status accounts for 43%
of the variance for this measure for the sample
of 309 women ($F(2,306) = 101.48$, $p < .0001$).

Table 26.   Sex of Person Closest to Subject
by Five Professional Groups

	Percent		
	Female	Male	Total
Home Economists	41	59	59
Doctors	23	77	47
Lawyers	21	79	38
Homemakers	10	90	68
Nurses	33	67	51
Total	25	75	263

Note. $X^2(4) = 17.59$, $p < .002$

$X^2(2) = 16.78, p < .0002$, show that home economists and nurses claim to have women as their closest friend most of the five groups (41% and 33% respectively). Homemakers (10%) have the least number of women closest friends. Directly related is the significant finding shown in Table 27 that the majority of women, 62%, cited their husband as their closest friend (full list of relationships in Appendix D). Homemakers (87%) report this person to be their husband most often and traditionals (42%) report husbands least often of the categories in the five-way, $p < .0001$, and three-way, $X^2(4) = 41.44, p < .0001$, analyses. The difference may be explained largely by the fact that more traditional women are single since home economists (34%) and nurses (40%) do report "lover/fiance, friend, colleague" (i.e., potential future husbands) very often.

In the open-ended section most often home economists (14 references) reported that "positive encouragement from a non-relative" (e.g., friend, housekeeper, therapist) was very important for their career development; in order following the home economist women in terms of experiencing positive encouragement from a non-relative were the doctors, lawyers, homemakers and nurses (8 references). A doctor writes, "I had thought I'd like to be a nurse, but with the encouragement of my college counselor I decided to apply to medical school and become a doctor like my mother. She assured me I had what it would take." Of all the women, only two doctors reported having experienced discouragement from a peer and only one home economist discussed a non-relative who was a negative role model.

Table 27. Relationship of Person Closest to Subject by Five Professional Groups

	Husband	Lover/Fiance Friend Colleague	"Other" Relative	Total N
		Percent		
Home Economists	44	34	22	59
Doctors	68	17	15	47
Lawyers	63	21	16	38
Homemakers	87	1	12	69
Nurses	40	40	19	52
TOTAL	62	22	17	265

Note. $X^2(8) = 42.41, p < .0001$

Summary

Several environment variables distinguish the groups from each other. The two childhood hobbies chosen most by each group were: sports and reading by doctors, lawyers and homemakers, domestic activities and sports by nurses and home economists. A childhood sex appropriate orientation towards activities was reported more by the professionals than the homemakers. As adults, all of the groups of women chose their same hobbies except for homemakers who now prefer domestic activities and sports.

Expectation 10, i.e., that nontraditional women more often remain single, or if they get married, have fewer children, received mixed support. All groups of women except nurses reported "married" as their modal response to the question of marital status. Of the single subjects, the largest number were nurses. Homemakers and doctors have been married the longest of the groups; nurses the shortest. Although "no children" was the modal response for traditional and nontraditional women, the nontraditional women had significantly more children than the traditional women. Homemakers had the most children. Doctors were the oldest to give birth to their first child. Nontraditional women were the most committed to their present marital/career situations which they described as "combining marriage and childrearing with employment" (#14). Homemakers reported the most "regrets" with their present life situations; home economists never referred to any regrets. In high school and college, homemakers were more oriented towards marriage and children than the professionals and nontraditional women who were the most non-traditionally career oriented. Homemakers commented that their family responsibility limited their career plans most often of the groups; home economists, doctors and lawyers reported problems resulting from family responsibilities least often. "Family obligations," in fact, positively influenced home economists the most with their career plans. Whereas the majority of all women sampled chose a man as their closest friend, traditional women had proportionately the largest number of closest friends who were women; homemakers reported the largest proportion of men friends (husband). Home economists reported the most and homemakers the least "positive encouragement from a nonrelative" as important to their career development.

Self Characteristic Variables

The few "self" variables asking questions directly about the women include those about her age, height and weight, (positive) self-image as a child (Factor 1), (positive) present self image (Factor 8) and perceptions of self-discipline and planning (Factor 10) as well as characteristics about the women elicited in the open-ended portion.

Tables 20 and 21 show that a MANOVA contrasting the five groups on age, height and weight self variables (and environment variables of number of children subject has and commitment to present marital/career situation) resulted in a significant overall group difference, $F(20,916) = 8.88$, $p < .001$. Data from these tables also show that MANOVAs resulted in significant differences when comparing all professionals with homemakers, $F(5,276) = 18.37$, $p < .001$, and nontraditionals with traditionals, $F(5,276) = 9.58$, $p < .001$.

Data from Tables 20 and 21 also show that an ANOVA indicated that the nontraditional women sampled were significantly older than the traditional women, $F(5,276) = 19.55$, $p < .001$. Table 1 presents the modal and mean age for each group. Briefly, doctors and homemakers were the oldest groups sampled, home economists and nurses the youngest groups. Expectation 12 (that nontraditional career women perceive themselves as more attractive), Expectation 11 (that nontraditional career women perceive themselves as more intelligent), and Expectation 14 (that nontraditional career women perceive themselves as stronger) were not supported by the data. Expectation 13 (that nontraditional women perceive themselves as taller) receives some support. Although chi square analysis of women's height did not result in any significant differences, the most women falling into the tallest category were the lawyers (26%), followed by the home economists, nurses, doctors and homemakers (15%); and the most women falling into the shortest category were the doctors (28%), the other groups were 19% and lower. Tables 3 and 4 show a trend difference, $F(1,263) = 3.70$, $p < .055$, and suggests that nontraditional women had a more "positive self image as a child" (Factor 1) than the traditional women.

In the open-ended section, doctors (22 responses), as a group, were the ones who most often cited their career development as having been influenced by positive characteristics of themselves. Such thoughts as "I knew I was bright—self determined—from the beginning of life I always felt I was special and could do whatever I wanted—I worked very hard—ambitious—my independence, self-confidence, the fact that I am outgoing and like and get along with people" were expressed. Home economists (18 references) followed (seven of these responses came from Ph.D. holders); then lawyers (10 references) and nurses (10 references) and last homemakers (8 references; one from a Ph.D. holder). Homemakers, on the other hand, offered the most (9 references) "negative self-characteristics" as having hindered their career development, e.g., "I was fascinated by science but afraid to pursue it—I was a passive child; I did what my parents told me and was unhappy." "*My poor opinion of myself as a child* hindered me for years. Sometimes I still wonder if my brain is made of cold oatmeal. I never learned to study. I feel I have gotten over most of my childhood hangups but alas, insight and self esteem have come so late. I'm 49. There is still time to do something for myself but I'll never accomplish now what I could have if I had had a better start in life." Nurses were second in suggesting these negative characteristics and lawyers, home economists and doctors (1 reference) similarly made very few references to negative characteristics. "Physical sickness" of oneself was also cited as positively affecting some of the women's career development. Nurses (6 references) reported "sickness" the most of the five groups, followed by homemakers and doctors (2 references), home economists and lawyers made no references to "sickness."

Summary

Doctors and homemakers were the oldest groups sampled; home economists and nurses the youngest groups. (Expectation 11–Expectation 14). Previous research indicated that the nontraditional career women would perceive themselves as more intelligent, more attractive, taller and stronger than other women. The data do not confirm the expected differences, although there is some data which suggests differences. For example, consistent with expectations was a trend suggesting that nontraditional women had a more positive self-image as a child than traditional women. In addition, in the open-ended section, doctors as a group were the ones who most often cited their career development as having been positively influenced by positive self-characteristics. Homemakers, on the other hand, offered the most negative self-characteristics as having hindered their career development. The height expectation was supported only by the lawyers who, proportionately, had the most women in the "tallest" category. Physical sickness most positively affected nurses' career development.

Within Career Category Differences

Doctors and Lawyers

Although only a few significant differences were found within the nontraditional group comparisons relative to the five group comparisons, the differences suggested between doctors and lawyers warrant discussion. Tables 3 and 4 show that MANOVAs of the 10 factors support that doctors are significantly different from lawyers, $F(10,254) = 4.85$, $p < .0001$.

Tables 5 and 6 show that MANOVA of the subgroup *employment variables* supports this significant difference, $F(3,289) = 2.91$, $p < .035$. Figure 1 shows that chi square analysis demonstrates that doctors (52%) have been employed in their present jobs significantly longer, 6–50 years, $X^2(4) = 14.51$, $p < .0006$, than lawyers (24%). This difference may be accounted for by the fact that doctors are older than lawyers (see p. 000). Tables 5 and 6 show that ANOVA results suggest that lawyers held more jobs during high school than doctors, $F(1,291) = 4.37, p < .038$, and lawyers' jobs were in more fields than doctors, $F(1,291) = 4.90, p < .028$. Table 7 shows that doctors (44%) left their jobs slightly more often, $X^2(1) = 3.40, p < .065$, than lawyers (24%) for more desirable positions; and Table 7 shows that significantly more, $X^2(1) = 5.8, p < .016$, because they had a position which ended when they earned their degree (doctors = 32%, lawyers = 9%). Table 7 shows that lawyers (29%) left their jobs significantly more often than doctors (7%) for the stated reason of children, family or pregnancy, $X^2(1) = 6.33, p < .012$.

When discussing their employment history and how it effected their career development in the open-ended section, doctors (23 references) responded with no explanation—"I have always wanted to be in this profession"—much more often than lawyers (12 references). Data from Table 3 and 4 show that lawyers reported having been positively influenced by their "political activism" (Factor 7) significantly more, $F(1,263) = 13.90, p < .001$ than doctors.

In terms of *education variables,* only three variables distinguish doctors from lawyers. Table 11 shows that a trend, $X^2(1) = 3.44, p < .064$, is suggested from chi square analysis for lawyers (53%) discontinuing their education more often than doctors (35%). College majors were significantly different for the two groups of nontraditional women. Tables 32 and 34 (in Appendix G) show that more often, lawyers majored in political science, $p < .0001$, and doctors in science, $X^2(4) = 170.30, p < .0001$ (Appendix G). In addition, these women reported on some different influencers in the open-ended portion of the questionnaire. Whereas two lawyers remembered their all women's college environment as having been supportive of their education, two doctors remembered their college environment as being more conducive to socializing than studying. On the other hand, doctors (18 references) referred to positive encouragement from education people much more than the lawyers (8 references). Only two lawyers and no doctors made references to books, documents, t.v., or movies which positively influenced their career plans.

Only a few *family variables* resulted in significant differences. Tables 16 and 17 show that chi square analysis of the ages 5–18 years suggest that doctors (21%) had significantly more mothers, $X^2(2) = 11.61, p < .003$, than lawyers (2%) who were professionals and doctors' fathers (49%), $X^2(3) = 8.30, p < .040$, were more often professionals than lawyers (36%) whereas the lawyers' fathers (23%) more often were managers and administrators than doctors' fathers (9%). Table 19 shows that chi square analysis of religious background resulted in significant differences, $X^2(2) = 6.88, p < .032$, with lawyers representing a larger proportion of Jewish backgrounds (30%) than doctors (13%) and doctors (65%) having more of a Protestant background than lawyers (19%). Data from Tables 3 and 4 show that an ANOVA found that lawyers report having perceived their relationship with their parents (Factor 6) as significantly more negative than doctors, $F(1,263) = 6.61, p < .011$. In response to the open-ended questions referring to significant others, doctors (17 references) more than lawyers (6 references) recalled positive family role models (most often the subject's mother) whom they emulated; lawyers (6 references) more than doctors (3 references) recalled negative role models (usually the subject's mother) whom they did not want to become like. It was only some doctors who suggested that their "family constellation" or "moving often" had positively influenced their career decisions.

Analysis of *environmental variables* resulted in several significant differences. Data from Tables 20 and 21 show that MANOVA of the subgroup environmental (and self) variables supported this significant difference between doctors and lawyers, $F(5,276) = 7.48, p < .001$. Tables 22 and 28 show that doctors were significantly more interested in "domestic activities" (32%), $X^2(1) = 6.22, p < .013$, and nature activities (15%), $p < .008$ than lawyers (10%, 3% respectively) as a child. Tables 3 and 4 show that an ANOVA supports this with the finding that doctors reported a sex appropriate orientation (Factor 9) significantly more than lawyers, $F(1,263) = 15.53, p < .001$. Table 23 shows that, with respect to present hobbies, lawyers (66%) participated in sports significantly more often than doctors (43%), $X^2(1) = 3.98, p < .046$, and doctors (34%) are somewhat more often involved in domestic activities than lawyers (17%), $X^2(1) = 3.11, p < .078$. Table 24 presents results of chi square analysis that demonstrate that doctors (70%) are more often married than lawyers (57%), $X^2(2) = 6.19, p < .045$. Data from Tables 20 and 21 show that ANOVAs indicate that doctors have significantly more children, $F(1,280) = 5.35, p < .021$, and are more committed, $F(1,280) = 4.27, p < .040$, to their present marital and career situations. Data from Tables 3 and 4 show that in addition to their marital preferences, ANOVA results suggest that doctors are somewhat more, $F(1,263) = 3.82, p < .052$, oriented towards nontraditional careers (Factor 4) throughout their high school and college days. Open-ended responses suggest that only doctors (2 references) experienced discouragement from a peer.

Table 28.   Childhood Hobby—Nature
Activities—By Doctors and Lawyers

	Percent		
	NO	YES	TOTAL N
Doctors	70	30	50
Lawyers	93	7	40
TOTAL	80	20	90

Note. $X^2(1) = 7.03, p < .008$

Data from Tables 20 and 21 show that ANOVA contrasts of *self variables* suggest that doctors are significantly older, $F(1,280) = 30.93$, $p < .001$, that lawyers are taller, $F(1,280) = 5.44$, $p < .020$, and that lawyers have a more positive self image (Factor 8), $F(1,263) = 3.84$, $p < .051$. More doctors (22 references) than lawyers (10 references) however, reported positive self-characteristics as having influenced their career development in the open-ended section.

Home Economists and Nurses

The traditional women also report differences in their background which warrant discussion. Tables 3 and 4 show that ANOVA contrasts of home economists and nurses resulted in significant differences for all the factors, $F(10,254) = 2.14$, $p < .022$.

The only information which significantly distinguishes the two groups in terms of *employment variables* relates to reasons for leaving their jobs and participation in volunteer groups. Table 7 shows that home economists (41%) significantly more than nurses (8%), $X^2(1) = 15.62$, $p < .0001$, left "for more school" whereas nurses (45%) more than home economists (5%) left, $X^2(1) = 22.92$, $p < .0001$, because they were dissatisfied with their jobs. Data from Tables 3 and 4 show that home economists participated in significantly more volunteer groups (Factor 5) than nurses, $F(1,263) = 7.48$, $p < .007$. Open-ended responses suggest a few more differences. Nurses (22 responses) attributed "characteristics of the job" as having positively influenced their career plans much more often than home economists (7 responses). Home economists (21 responses), on the other hand, reported the "always wanted to be" a home economist more than the nurses (14 responses). Home economics women (19 references), more often than nurses (7 references) recalled positive influence from non-related role models in their field.

Tables 9 and 10 show that MANOVA of the *education variables* resulted in an overall significant difference between home economists and nurses, $F(11,232) = 7.35$, $p < .001$. Table 11 shows that chi square analysis indicates that home economists (63%) had discontinued their education significantly more than nurses (22%), $X^2(1) = 21.19$, $p < .0001$. One possible explanation of why home economists discontinued their education more is that they often went on for advanced degrees; i.e., this break may refer to time between college and graduate school. Tables 9 and 10 show that an ANOVA of education variables also resulted in significant differences, $F(11,232) = 7.35$, $p < .001$; nurses had higher high school grades, $F(1,242) = 5.84$, $p < .016$. Tables 9 and 10 also show that in college, $F(1,242) = 12.67$, $p < .001$, and at present, $F(1,242) = 14.60$, $p < .001$, home economists participated in more organizations and were leaders more often than nurses. Tables 33 and 34 (in Appendix G) indicate that chi square analysis also show obvious significant differences in college majors.

Seventy-nine percent of the home economists majored in home economics, $X^2(1) = 79.34, p < .0001$, and 95% of the nurses in nursing, $X^2(1) = 106.61, p < .0001$. Tables 13, 29 and 30 show that differences were also found in terms of how these women financed their education. Chi square analysis suggests that more often nurses (nurses = 71%, home economists = 54%) financed their education through support from their parents, $X^2(1) = 3.95, p < .047$ and loans or borrowing (nurses = 24%, home economists = 11%), $X^2(1) = 3.87, p < .049$ whereas home economists (home economists = 15%, nurses = 2%) used savings, $p < .007$ and more often worked (home economists = 71%, nurses = 47%), $X^2(1) = 7.45, p < .006$ and had somewhat more financial backing from their husbands (home economists = 12%, nurses = 3%), $p < .069$. Only home economists (11 responses) reported, in the open-ended section, that financial aid, particularly assistantships, positively influenced their career decisions.

Table 29. Subjects Reporting Financed Their
Education Through Their "Savings"
by Home Economists and Nurses

	Percent		
	NO	YES	TOTAL N
Home Economists	85	15	65
Nurses	98	2	59
TOTAL	91	9	124

Note. $X^2(1) = 7.17$, $p < .007$

Table 30. Subjects Reporting Financed Their
Education by Their "Husband"
by Home Economists and Nurses

	Percent		
	NO	YES	TOTAL N
Home Economists	88	12	65
Nurses	97	3	59
TOTAL	92	8	124

Note. $X^2(1) = 3.32$, $p < .069$

Several other open-ended responses resulted in differences between these two categories. Home economists (31 responses) more often than nurses (7 responses) suggested that previous interests and classes had positively influenced them; only nurses (3 references) recalled books, t.v. or movies. Whereas only nurses (3 responses) remembered that the college environment (in particular an all women's college was mentioned) was supportive of her career development, only home economists (2 references) wrote that the college environment was not facilitative of academic achievement. In direct contrast to this are the large number of home economists (22 references) more than nurses (3 references) who recalled many faculty who encouraged them "I received much encouragement by previous professors who *expressed* faith in my abilities and pushed me to do my best in their classes and to continue to do so *after* graduation." Only nurses (3 references) recalled discouragement. "Probably my lack of self-confidence, which my father and teacher reinforced was the biggest influence on my career. I feel now I had the potential to go to medical school or into math, but did poorly in these classes."

Nurses and home economists differed somewhat in terms of *family background variables*. Although no significant difference was established by a chi square analysis of mother's occupation, frequency tables showed that five nurses had mothers in the same field whereas no home economists had mothers in their same field of work. Table 17 shows that fathers' occupations resulted in significant differences throughout the subject's life, $X^2(3) = 11.62, p < .009$. Home economists' (36%) fathers most often were farmers and nurses' (43%) fathers were most often employed in "other"—a wide variety of occupations. Table 31 shows that of the single women, home economists (46%) lived with another person significantly more often than nurses (27%), $p < .028$. Home economists also offered some other variables in the open-ended section of the questionnaire, which they felt positively influenced their career plans. "Encouragement from a relative" was cited much more often by home economists (48 references) than nurses (26 references). For example, one home economist writes, "My husband has been very cooperative in the planning of my career. He was supportive (both financially and positively) in college and he is encouraging me to find a job that I like and that I feel I can progress." "Family constellation" or the "opportunity to leave a small town" were only related by home economists (5 references).

Several *environmental variables* resulted in significant differences within the traditional group. Data from Tables 20 and 21 show that MANOVA of the subgroup environmental (and self) variables supports this significant difference, $F(5,276) = 3.92, p < .0002$. Table 22 shows that chi square analyses indicate that home economists (57%) significantly more often than nurses (37%) chose domestic activities, $X^2(4) = 25.47, p < .0001$ as a childhood hobby. Table 23 shows that presently, nurses participate in arts and crafts (nurses = 35%, home economists = 16%), $X^2(1) = 4.87, p < .027$, and sports (nurses =

Table 31.   Person Lived With the Subject's
Family When She Was a Child

	Percent		
	NO	YES	TOTAL N
Home Economists	54	46	65
Nurses	73	27	59
TOTAL	63	37	124

Note. $X^2(1)$ = 4.80, p < .028

71%, home economists = 46%), $X^2(1) = 6.71, p < .010$, more often and home economists in domestic activities (home economists = 64%, nurses = 45%), $X^2(1) = 3.97, p < .046$. Figure 3 shows that chi square analyses support that home economists have been married significantly longer (mode = 11–20 years) than nurses (mode = 5 years or less), $X^2(3) = 17.62, p < .001$. Data from Tables 20 and 21 show that ANOVAs suggest that home economists are somewhat more committed to their present marital/career situations than nurses, $F(1,280) = 3.38, p < .067$. Home economists, in fact, reported more often (home economists = 10 references, nurses = 5 references) in the open-ended section that family responsibilities had positively influenced their career plans whereas nurses more often (nurses = 11 references, home economists = 6 references) felt family responsibility hindered their careers. One nurse expresses her difficulties, "Being a single parent often requires so much energy: 1) support family—work hard, keep job 2) parent children 3) meet own needs— there is little energy left to pursue future goals at this time." Data from Tables 3 and 4 indicate that ANOVAs show that nurses were somewhat more nontraditionally career oriented (Factor 4) than the home economists, $F(1,263) = 3.05, p < .082$. The open-ended responses suggested that home economists (14 responses) recalled, more than nurses (8 responses), having been influenced by positive encouragement from a non-relative.

Data from Tables 20 and 21 show that MANOVA of home economists with nurses in terms of *self variables* resulted in a significant difference, $F(5,276) = 3.92, p < .002$. Home economists were significantly older than nurses, $F(1,280) = 17.67, p < .001$. Tables 3 and 4 show that home economists had a more positive self image as a child (Factor 1), $F(1,263) = 4.67, p < .032$. In addition, in the open-ended section, home economists (18 references) more often than nurses (10 references) cited positive self-characteristics as having influenced them and nurses (5 references) more than home economists (2 references) reported negative self-characteristics as having hindered their career development. One nurse illustrates her self-doubts by writing "I was frightened out of pursuing medicine by the knowledge at that time (1957-60) that only females with extremely high GPA would be accepted in medical school—I doubted my ability to succeed and got encouragement from family and friends to pursue nursing not medicine."

4

Discussion

Summary of Results Relevant to Expectations

Employment Variables

(*E1*)   It was expected that nontraditional professional women would be more likely to have experienced a larger number and wider variety of previous jobs than other women. The results provide only partial support for this expectation. The data suggest that professional women, particularly home economists, held the largest number of jobs after high school, but homemakers' jobs reflected the most variety. In high school, lawyers reported the largest number of jobs and home economists the smallest number. Traditional women, most often, left their jobs to move or to accept a more desirable position. Homemakers left because of marriage and pregnancy. No reason was given consistently more by doctors or lawyers, though doctors and lawyers least often report having had previous negative job experiences. Doctors, in fact, were least influenced by their past jobs since they stated they "had always wanted to be in this profession" more than the other women. Qualitative data obtained from open-ended questions suggest that it was the traditional women whose careers were most positively influenced by their previous jobs; nontraditional women were least influenced by their employment history.

(*E2*)   Data on nontraditional women, particularly the lawyers, supports the expectation that nontraditional women experienced a women's (support) group and perceived this experience as having positively influenced their career development more than traditional women. Homemakers also stated that volunteer participation in all women's groups, especially the League of Women Voters, had supported their present careers as well as encouraged them to take on leadership roles and consider the possibility of part-time employment.

Another employment related variable not previously explored emerged from the study. Societal issues such as the Women's Movement or the Depression seemed to have influenced nontraditional women more than the other women, although this did not emerge as a major factor influencing career choice.

Education Variables

(*E3*) It was expected that pioneer women, more than other women, have received positive support from a professor or other influential role model during their college and post-college training. The data suggest a trend in this direction. Qualitative data obtained from open-ended questions suggest that, as expected, more nontraditional women were influenced by a role model during their college and post-college training. In terms of encouragement, however, larger numbers of the traditional home economists and nontraditional doctors credited school related people with having supported their career aspirations.

Several other education related variables new to this study were explored. Nontraditional women earned the highest grades in high school and college. Although the majority of all women reported "parents" and "working" as sources of financial support, homemakers cited finances as having presented problems with their career plans; nontraditional women never mentioned financial problems interfering with their career plans. In high school, homemakers participated in the most organizations, nontraditionals the least. Of all the groups of women, home economists recalled being most positively influenced by previous interests and classes, homemakers by group experiences and nurses and lawyers by college environments (particularly all women's colleges).

Family Variables

(*E4*) It was expected that nontraditional women, more often than other women, were reared by employed mothers. The results provide only partial support. Of all the groups, nurses and doctors had the largest number of employed mothers, lawyers were among the lowest. Homemakers had the most full-time homemakers for mothers.

(*E5*)   In addition, it was expected and the data supports that the mothers of nontraditional women were in nontraditional careers more often than other women's mothers. Proportionately, nontraditional women, particularly the doctors, did have more mothers in nontraditional careers with advanced degrees than other women. Whereas these employed mothers positively influenced the doctors, they negatively influenced homemakers and lawyers. Data on father's occupation, another variable not systematically explored before, showed that nontraditional women, particularly the doctors, had the most fathers who were professionals, occasionally in their same occupations.

(*E6, E7, E8*)   It was expected that nontraditional women more than other women were likely to be first borns, without male siblings, and to have perceived their childhood relationships with their mothers as more hostile than nurturant. None of these expectations were confirmed. However, significantly more lawyers than doctors perceived their childhood relationships with their mothers as hostile.

(*E9*)   As expected, more of the nontraditional women, particularly the lawyers, came from Jewish families; contrary to expectations, however, these nontraditional women also had more Catholic backgrounds than the other groups.

New information generated by the subjects suggest differences among the groups of women. Reactions from relatives encouraged homemakers to continue with their homemaking career plans but discouraged them from seriously considering employment outside the home. Doctors and nurses most often recalled "sickness" of a family member or close significant other as having positively influenced their career decision.

Environmental Variables

(*E10*)   It was expected that, more than other groups, the nontraditional career women remained single, and that if they were married, they had fewer children. For the most part, the data do not support this expectation. The modal response for all of the groups of women except nurses was "married" and significantly more homemakers and doctors were married, had been married a longer period of time and had more children than the other groups of women. The nurses were most often single. Several new environmental variables were investigated and suggest differences among the groups of women. Doctors were the oldest to give birth to their first child. Nontraditional women were the most committed to their present marital/career situations which, contrary to expectations, they described as "combining marriage and childrearing with employment." Homemakers reported the most regrets with their present life situations and home economists never referred to any regrets. Consistent with expectations, nontraditional women were the most nontraditionally career-oriented throughout high school and college, homemakers were the most marriage and family-oriented. Whereas homemakers commented that their family responsibilities limited their career plans, home economists suggested that family obligations positively influenced their career decisions. Traditional women presently had the largest number of closest friends who were women, homemakers reported the most men. Positive encouragement from a relative most influenced home economists and least influenced homemakers. Doctors, lawyers and homemakers enjoyed reading and sports most as children, home economists and nurses enjoyed domestic activities and sports.

Self-Characteristic Variables

(*E11–E14*)   Previous research indicated that the nontraditional career women would perceive themselves as more intelligent, more attractive, taller and stronger than other women. The data do not confirm the expected differences, although there is some data which suggests differences. For example, consistent with expectations was a trend suggesting that nontraditional women had a more positive self-image as a child than traditional women. In addition, in the open-ended section, doctors as a group were the ones who most often cited their career development as having been positively influenced by positive self-characteristics. Homemakers, on the other hand, offered the most negative self-characteristics as having hindered their career development. The height expectation was supported only by the lawyers who, proportionately, had the most women in the "tallest" category.

Descriptions of the Five Groups of Women

The group differences presented in the results chapter suggest certain modal patterns of career development that characterize doctors, lawyers, home economists, nurses and homemakers. Recognizing that there are exceptions, the following descriptions will present portraits of typical women in each group.

Doctors

The typical doctor in this study is Caucasian, in her 40's, somewhat smaller than average height (5'4" or less) and weighs around 135 pounds. She was reared by both of her Protestant parents, and her family constellation is similar to women in general. Compared to other traditional and homemaking women in this study, however, she is more likely to have been reared in a Jewish or Catholic family. Her mother, although probably a homemaker, was more likely than the other women's mothers to be employed in a nontraditional profession, particularly medicine. The typical doctor's mother did not finish college, but a minority (more than other women) have earned an advanced degree. Her father was a professional. Her parents typically offered encouragement for her career decisions.

Throughout her life, the typical doctor enjoyed sports and reading. As a child she often played with girls, felt positively about herself, and now remembers being somewhat feminine. She began dating when she was 17 years old. She is presently married, has been married for at least 10 years and has one or two children. Her first child was not born until she was over 30 years of age. She is strongly committed to her life of marriage, childrearing and employment and expresses few regrets. Though she presently considers her husband her closest friend, throughout college and medical school she had more women than men friends. In addition to the support she receives from her parents and husband, this woman depends on assistance from others, such as her housekeeper and only rarely can she recall discouragement from a peer.

In high school and college this doctor earned very high grades (A/B+) majoring in science, and slightly lower grades in medical school, B average. She has consistently been oriented towards a nontraditional career, and more than the other women sampled, the typical doctor recalls having always wanted to be in this profession. She earned her medical degree when she was 25 years old. She has not participated in many organizations, only one or two, nor held many leadership positions throughout high school, college, medical school or at present. If she is part of the 35% who discontinued their education, she probably did not leave her studies for more than one year, and it was most likely for employment. She financed her education from various sources, including support from her parents, working, earning scholarships or fellowships, loans from the university or borrowing from individuals. She did not experience her financial situation as limiting her career development. More than other professionals, this woman remembers a significant role model and received much encouragement from significant others in her educational environment. Also more than other women, she may recall religion, sickness of a significant other or societal issues as having positively influenced her career plans.

The typical doctor's employment as well as educational background reflects a steady progression towards a medical career. She has been employed in her present position at least six years. She had one job during high school and several jobs since high school, mostly in the medical field. She reports leaving a job most often for a more desirable position, although she also may have left to continue her formal education because her job was not rewarding enough, or because the position was held in conjunction with earning a degree. This doctor almost never remembers negative job experiences and has not left a job because of marriage or pregnancy.

Lawyers

Typically, the lawyer in this study is Caucasian, in her early 30's, is taller than most other women sampled (at least 5'5") and weighs around 130 pounds. Although she is most likely Protestant, compared to the other groups of women she is more likely to be Jewish or possibly Catholic. Her self image is positive and she remembers more positive than negative qualities about herself. Although she was probably reared by both parents, her mother was more likely than the other women's mothers to have died before she was five years old. Her mother was most likely a homemaker with a high school degree, not employed outside of her home. Her father was a professional with a college degree and, more likely than the other women's fathers, he was in her field, law. Relative to most other women, she perceives her relationship with her parents as negative, she recalls more negative familial role models and received less encouragement from them for her career plans.

This typical lawyer continues to like sports and reading. She started dating when she was 17 years old. She has been married about 6-10 years and gave birth to her one and perhaps only child in her late 20's. Her commitment to her marriage, children and employment is strong. Her closest friend is her husband and she has always had proportionately more men than women friends compared to other women in this sample. Though she does not recall much encouragement from her relatives, she does recall positive encouragement from friends and other non-relatives as having been important for her career decisions.

The typical lawyer received her law degree when she was 25 years old, discontinuing her education for about a year. She earned very high grades in high school (A) and college (A/ B+), while probably majoring in political science and good grades in law school (B). Her parents were her main source of financial support; she also worked, and more than other women, took loans and borrowed to finance her education. Like doctors, she was nontraditionally career-oriented and did not join many organizations thoughout her life. She did, however, participate in more women's political groups than the other women. Books, t.v., movies or a women's college positively influenced her career plans more than most of the other groups of women. During school, she experienced more role models who were educators and encouragement than traditional women or homemakers.

The typical lawyer's employment as well as educational background reflects a progression towards a nontraditional career, though not necessarily a career in law. She has been employed in her present position two to three years. She held one to two jobs during high school (more than other high school girls in this sample) and has had quite a few jobs since high school, some of which have been in fields other than law. Although she probably did not leave any positions because of marriage, she may have left because of pregnancy or children. Characteristics of the job, such as prestige, ability to afford material comforts, or potential for social change may have positively influenced her career decisions and more than other traditional or homemaking women sampled, societal issues such as the Women's Movement or the Depression may have positively influenced her career development.

Home Economists

The typical home economist is Caucasian, Protestant, in her mid 30's, somewhat above the average height (5'5") and weighs about 137 pounds. Her self-image is relatively positive. Although brought up by both of her parents, her father was more likely than nontraditional or homemaker's fathers to have died when she was a young child. Her mother was a homemaker with a high school degree. Her father was a farmer or other non-professional with less than a high school education (less education than the fathers of the other groups of women). There is a good possibility that someone other than her immediate family members lived with her family during her childhood. In addition to considering a family member as a positive role model, she recalls much encouragement from her parents or other relative for her career development.

As a child, she enjoyed domestic activities more than other girls her age. Along with other girls, however, she also participated in sports throughout her life. She began dating at 15 and has most likely been married for over 10 years. She has one child and gave birth when she was 26–29 years old. Reporting no regrets with her life, she is committed to her life of marriage, childrearing and employment. Family responsibilities, in fact, may have encouraged her to resume her career plans. Of all the groups of women, home economists typically have had the most women friends. Presently, she has more women friends than other groups of women but probably considers her husband or future husband the person closest to her. Of all the women, she recalls the most positive encouragement from a non-relative such as a friend or therapist.

This woman probably earned a masters degree or Ph.D. She discontinued her education at least three years for employment and received her higher degree at a somewhat older age than the other women sampled. Majoring in home economics, she earned good grades, B/B+, throughout her school years. For the most part, she wanted to be a home economist all of her life. This typical home economist, more than the other women, suggests that previous interests and classes, particularly 4-H activities, as well as encouragement from educators positively influenced her career development. She financed most of her education by working. Her parents also helped her, though less so than other women's parents. She considers the finances she received, such as scholarships, to have encouraged her to pursue an advanced degree. Her participation in organizations, around three, and leadership positions, two, throughout her life is similar to most other women.

Typically, this home economist has an employment as well as educational background which reflects several breaks in her career development upon completing college. Since returning to her career, this home economist has been employed in her present position over 6 years. Though she held the least number of jobs in high school of the women studied here, she has held the most jobs after high school (over four); some of these jobs have been in fields other than home economics. When leaving a position, she most often left because of dissatisfaction with her present position, the opportunity of a more desirable position, or to continue her formal education. She considers these previous job experiences as well as her volunteer experiences to have been positive influences on her career development, even though she did recall some negative job experiences. This typical home economist has received much positive encouragement from the people she worked with and of all the groups, she has experienced the most positive role models in her employment field.

Nurses

The typical nurse in this study is Caucasian, Protestant, in her late 20's (the youngest of the groups of women studied), average height (5'5") and weight (135). Her opinion of herself and her career development is somewhat more ambivalent than the self-image of other women professionals, reflecting both positive and negative self-characteristics. Though probably reared by both of her parents, her father was more likely than the nontraditional women or homemaker's fathers to have died when she was a young child. Of all the women, her mother was most likely to be employed, often as a professional, sometimes as a nurse. Her father was usually a non-professional (e.g., a carpenter or salesperson). Both of her parents earned high school degrees. This nurse, along with doctors, may have been influenced in her career plans by sickness of a close significant other or of herself. Though she recalls positive family role models, of all the groups of women, she remembers the least encouragement for her career from family members.

She has continued to participate in sports and domestic activities. She typically began dating around the age of 15 years and is probably unmarried. (If she is married, it has been for less than five years and she has one child.) This single nurse anticipates remaining employed before her children are born, then resuming employment after the birth of her last child. This anticipated change is reflected in her substantial commitment to her present life situation. She anticipates that family obligations, may however, hinder her career development. In high school and college, this nurse was more nontraditionally career-oriented than other traditional women or homemakers. More than the other groups of women studied, she has consistently had many women friends. The person presently closest to her is her male friend/lover (or her husband if she is married).

Typically, this nurse completed her undergraduate education in nursing at 22 years without a break and did not continue on for an advanced degree. If she did leave school, it was probably for employment. She received the lowest overall grades, B, of all the groups of women. She financed most of her education with her parents help, but also reported the most help of all the women from scholarships and fellowships and the least from working. Like most of the other women studied here, she participated in one or two organizations throughout her life and had few leadership positions. More so than the other women studied, books, t.v. or movies may have positively influenced her choice of a career and discouragement from educators may have negatively influenced her career plans.

She has been in her present job about one year. In high school, she held one job and since high school has had several different jobs, mostly in the nursing field. Upon leaving a job, the reason most often given was for a more desirable position, though she also often left because of dissatisfaction with her present position or moving. Of all the women, the nurse's career plans were most positively influenced by characteristics of the job (e.g., hours mesh with her home life, the chance to work with people). The people she worked with encouraged her career development as a nurse.

Homemaker

The typical homemaker in this study is Caucasian, Protestant, in her early 40's with an average height and weight. Her self-image seems more negative than any of the other groups of women, since she may describe herself with more negative than positive characteristics. Typically she was raised by both of her parents. Like herself, her mother was also a full-time homemaker. Her mother earned a high school degree and served as a positive role model for her daughter. More than other women, homemakers saw employed mothers as negative role models not to be copied. Although her father often earned a professional degree, he was most often employed as a nonprofessional such as a craftsperson or salesperson. This typical homemaker received much encouragement from relatives, the most of all women in fact, to become a full-time homemaker. Also more than other women, she remembers more discouragement for entertaining thoughts of employment.

As a child, she enjoyed sports and reading and as an adult enjoys domestic activities and sports. She began dating at 15. This homemaker has been married at least 21 years, the longest of all the women, and has the most children, two or three. Since high school and through college she has been oriented towards marriage and children more than the other women and most likely remembers always wanting to be a full-time homemaker. Though she is somewhat strongly committed to her life as a full-time homemaker, she feels that these family obligations have kept her from pursuing any other career. Because of this, she reports the largest number of regrets of all the groups of women. In college, she had the most women friends of all the groups of women. Presently, the person closest to her is her husband.

Her formal education probably stopped with a bachelors degree when she was 22 years old. Most likely she finished her undergraduate degree without any breaks in her formal training. High school and college grades were moderately high, B/B+. Though she may have majored in a variety of disciplines, she probably graduated with a degree in education. More than the other women, this homemaker was financially supported by her parents, supplemented by employment. More than the other women, she feels that lack of finances hindered her career development. Her participation in organizations in high school was the highest (three or more) of all the groups of women. Previous group work such as assertiveness training or life-career planning may have positively influenced her thoughts on future employment more than the other women sampled.

Typically then this homemaker completed her college education and employment experiences to become a full-time homemaker. Though she usually assumed some employment during high school, she is presently not employed outside of her home and has experienced the smallest number of jobs, three, since she graduated from high school. These jobs were in a variety of fields. More than the other women, the homemaker recalls that her previous jobs sometimes served to deter her from future employment. In addition to being a homemaker, this woman typically spends time in volunteer activities. She views these volunteer activities as having positively reinforced her career decisions as well as increased her leadership and employment abilities. Though she may recall some workers whom she emulated, she (more than other women sampled) also regrets the lack of positive role models whom she would have liked to have learned from. In addition, more than the other women, the typical homemaker feels societal issues, such as lack of day care, have not been supportive of her career development.

Understanding the Findings

The descriptions of the five groups of variables and five groups of women suggest several major findings. Most obvious and consistent is the finding that more significant differences resulted for the five professional groups, doctors, lawyers, home economists, nurses, and homemakers than the three career categories, nontraditional, traditional and homemaker. This finding, that doctors are significantly different from lawyers and home economists are significantly different from nurses on several background variables, was not anticipated from previous research findings, which assumed similarity in background and used measures of expectation to study women by their nontraditional, traditional or homemaking orientation (Lemkau, 1979). The women in the present study seemed to follow role specifications particular to their profession rather than particular to "nontraditional women." Doctors, for example, who exhibited more sex role appropriate behavior as children than lawyers, went into the more nurturing profession of medicine. Although data on the specific area of medicine was not collected on this sample of doctors, research literature suggests that women doctors often end up in the most women-oriented nurturing fields of pediatrics and psychiatry (Lloyd, 1975). In addition, the field of medicine requires long term goal directed behaviors from the person. Most doctors have majored in science in college and have taken science courses in high school. Lawyers, on the other hand, can come from various educational backgrounds. Law does not require the same prior long term commitment as does the field of medicine. Perhaps, then, educational and occupational structures may have played at least as much a role in shaping the career development of these women as any other background variable (Holter, 1970; Oritz, 1975; Safilios-Rothchild, 1979).

The career development of these women may in fact be quite similar to the men in these fields. Research on men's career development has consistently surveyed men in their specific occupational field and developed vocational interest measures based on these results (Boring, 1973). Thus, until further large scale research examining professional women demonstrates that these differences do not exist within career categories, the present research suggests that these professional women should be studied with women in their particular profession as well as with women in their same nontraditional, traditional or homemaking category. In addition, the present study indicates that the use of the concept, nontraditional, traditional or homemaking-oriented to discuss backgrounds of women is based on non-supportable assumptions and therefore should be used cautiously in future studies.

Another unexpected finding which resulted from analyzing the five groups of women separately is that the backgrounds and present lives of women who enter nontraditional careers are not that different from women who enter traditional careers or homemaking careers and are therefore not significantly different from traditional sex-role norms. Doctors, for example, played with girls more than boys as children and perceived themselves as more feminine than the other groups of women. As adults, doctors are combining their instrumental and expressive roles by integrating their professional and homemaking careers. Doctors, in fact, never left their careers for the reason of marriage and only rarely left for children or family reasons. Doctors are somewhat different from the other women in that they gave birth to their first child later in life. Lawyers also assume instrumental and expressive roles by combining career with marriage. Lawyers are more similar to the other women in that they sometimes left their careers for marriage or children. The majority of women enjoyed sports, started dating around 15–17 years of age, are married, and presently report a man (their husband) as their closest friend; the majority of nurses, however, are single. In terms of their parents' educational and employment backgrounds, nontraditional women, particularly doctors, did experience the most highly educated nontraditional mothers. However, whereas nurses and doctors had the largest number of employed mothers, lawyers were among the lowest. Homemakers, followed by lawyers, had the most full-time homemakers for mothers. Nontraditional women, again mostly the doctors, had the most fathers who were professionals, in particular fathers who were in their same occupations. Data on family constellation backgrounds did not distinguish the women. Although qualitative data obtained from open-ended questions indicated that doctors and lawyers expressed somewhat more positive self-images, and statistical data showed that nontraditional women received higher grades than the other groups, no one group considered themselves significantly more or less attractive, intelligent or strong than the others as children or presently in the quantitative statistical analysis.

Even though lawyers have been involved in women's political groups more than the other groups, none of these groups of women presented themselves as ardent feminists actively trying to change the image or roles of women in society. For the most part, these women presented themselves as professionals within a specific discipline and not as "Professional Women" different from other women or different from their colleagues. Thus, this data suggests that the non-traditional women sampled do not perceive themselves as violating normative expectations of women in American society. Only rarely did a doctor or lawyer express any sense of alienation/rejection from her colleagues or peers or any sense of pride in having assumed a position within a traditionally male-dominated high status profession. According to the normative paradigm, social order is maintained since professional socialization has led these women to internalize the rules and consensus about expected behaviors by the majority of the members within their specific professional culture rather than the culture in general. This sense of acceptance is reflected in their lifestyle, which seems to integrate rather than compartmentalize their home and employment life. They are, in fact, the groups most committed to their present life/career situations. These data and other recent findings (Yogev, 1983; Lemkau, 1979; Beckman & Houser, 1979) indicate that the nontraditional career women, doctors and lawyers, are significantly different from other women and traditional sex-role norms only in terms of their present nontraditional employment, but not significantly different in terms of lifestyle or values.

If these five groups of women are more similar than different, are there any patterns of variables which support women becoming professionals, particularly in nontraditional careers? In terms of the specific variables tested, the most salient finding seems to be that the presence of both positive role models and encouragement throughout the woman's life is important to nontraditional career development (Heins, Hendricks & Martindale, 1982; Stake, 1981; Stake & Levitz, 1979; Kuther & Brogan, 1980; Houseknecht & Macke, 1981). Social learning theory (Bandura, 1969; Rotter, 1972), which assumes that social behaviors are largely developed through exposure to powerful and nurturant models and maintained by reinforcement contingencies, would explain this research finding. For example, more than the other groups, doctors, whose career development reflects the clearest progression toward a nontraditional profession, report the presence of nontraditional role models and positive encouragement from significant others throughout most of their lives. A doctor describes the consistent support she has received. "I am grateful to my wonderful mother for providing the role model, to my college counselor for encouraging me to reach for higher goals, and to my husband for his patience, encouragement, and support—without him and his enthusiasm I couldn't have combined both family and career successfully. And because of my mother, I think I have much less guilt about working and leaving my children than many other women. Since I grew up with a housekeeper I am comfortable having a good loving lady who takes care of the children and the house and lives in." Lawyers, then the home economists follow; homemakers report the least amount of nontraditional role models or encouragement for a non-homemaking career. Nontraditional women, particularly doctors, report as children having been reared by the most nontraditional mothers. Whereas doctors recalled the most positive family role models and positive encouragement, lawyers recalled more negative family role models and less encouragement for their career plans.

Social learning theorists also argue that parents serve as only one source of models, since learning is a continuous process in which new responses are acquired and existing repertoires of behaviors are modified, by both direct and vicarious experiences with a wide variety of actual or symbolic models. During their education, the data suggests that doctors and lawyers received the most positive exposure to a professor or other influential role-model. In terms of encouragement, however, larger numbers of the traditional home economists and nontraditional doctors credited school related people with having supported their career aspirations. Many of these home economists later resumed their education to earn masters and Ph.D.'s. Lawyers, more than other groups, experienced support from other women role models in their field in women's political groups. Thus, the social learning theory and this data suggest that exposure to and support from women in various instrumental roles throughout women's lives seem to expand perceptions of normative behavior for women. One homemaker's response clearly illustrates this. "My upbringing placed limitations on me that some other women have not had to deal with like not having a mother who worked and expectations of me that were very traditional... But now... I plan to get some vocational counseling soon and I hope things will become clearer for me. Last night I had a really neat experience of hearing (and talking to) a panel of women talk about careers/lifestyles. Many of them started careers late or changed careers midway. That encouraged me so much."

Feminists, on the other hand, would explain that the women's movement, with its emphasis on raising consciousnesses to question traditional assumptions about sex roles, is helping to increase women's participation in various careers (Frieze et al., 1978; Freeman, 1975, 1973). Lawyers, who were somewhat career-oriented but not as profession-specific-oriented as the doctors, came to law from various fields. Having typically discontinued their education for about a year, feminists would argue that participation in women's political groups may have influenced lawyers' decisions to enter this nontraditional career. The present data concerning women's participation in women's support groups and their perceptions of the experience is limited, since support groups and women's caucuses in the professions (Plas & Wallston, 1983; Young, MacKenzie & Sherif, 1980, Carden, 1974; Hole & Levine, 1973) are a somewhat recent phenomenon. Many of the women sampled in the present study were established in their careers before the onset of support groups. Therefore, the number of women sampled who could have participated in such a group during their career development is quite small. The lawyers in this study, who were younger than the doctors, do report significantly more than the other groups the positive effects of their participation in women's political groups. This finding reflects a change from past research, which suggested that women lawyers do not want to associate with other women lawyers for fear of being regarded as a woman rather than a lawyer (Epstein, 1971b). Thus, future studies need to sample younger women, who would show more of the effects of support groups, before any conclusion can be made about the influence of feminist ideology and activities on women's career development.

It is possible that the nontraditional women, more than the other women, had opportunities such as their higher socioeconomic status (as demonstrated by their parents' higher educational and employment backgrounds) available to them which positively influenced their nontraditional career development. In addition, opportunities such as housekeepers helped the doctors and finances helped the home economists maintain their careers, whereas the absence of such childcare help or financial assistance limited the homemaker's career possibilities. The stereotype of the "homemaker—stuck at home," which was somewhat supported by the data is more true of lower middle and middle class women. As quoted earlier, one lawyer's response about the importance of money reiterates that upper middle class women can afford to not be "stuck," i.e., to further their education, be involved in clubs, or whatever they choose. Thus, though women in a more "privileged" class must still perform behaviors typical of the female role, activities external to their homelife are not perceived as particularly deviant. In addition, because these women have enjoyed the privileges associated with their social class throughout their lives, aspiring to the status and wealth associated with male dominated professions is not as foreign to them as it would be to a woman from a lower class, who is aspiring to a new status with new norms and roles. Because almost no other evidence is available from the data to support or refute this theoretical perspective, the role "opportunities" play in explaining women's career development should be explored in future research.

Another important area distinguishing the women seems to reflect the women's attitudes about themselves. As children, doctors felt the most positive about themselves. Qualitative data from the open-ended questions suggest that more nontraditional women than other women, particularly doctors, seem to attribute their career development to positive-characteristics of themselves. Home economists and nurses seem to express more of a mixture of positive and negative self-characteristics and homemakers express the most negative characteristics of themselves.

The data suggest that specific factors may be a necessary but not sufficient condition for nontraditional career development and that the more important variable may be the woman's reaction to the presence of these factors. For example, both nontraditional women and homemakers reported being reared with mothers who were employed in nontraditional fields. However, in the open-ended section discussing significant persons in the woman's life, different reactions to the same situation occurred. Whereas several of the doctors reported respecting their mothers and wanting to grow up to be like them ("My mother's medical background gave me an early committment to a medical career, and her own drive and investment provided a model for me") some homemakers recalled missing their nontraditional mothers as children, not receiving enough attention and not wanting to do the same thing to their own children. ("By going into business, my mother lost some of the benefits of a happy marriage and we kids lost out.") Were the mother/daughter interactions significantly different, or were the daughter's reactions to similar situations qualitatively different? Research on Rational Emotive Therapy (Ellis, 1962; Hymen, 1977) would point to the latter idea, that the daughters have different beliefs about and therefore different reactions to similar situations. Another example of differing reactions was to the "societal issues" (e.g., the climate of the 60's, the Depression, the Women's Movement) only offered by the nontraditional women as positive influencers on their career development. Several of the subjects lived through the Depression, or the 60's era, yet nontraditional women reported them as having positively affected their careers and homemakers negatively affecting their non-homemaking careers. Whereas some home economists felt their family responsibilities and financial situations had encouraged them to continue with their careers, homemakers commented that their family and financial situations limited their career choices. Doctors and lawyers report that their careers were neither encouraged nor discouraged by their family and financial situations.

Several other variables warrant comment. Significantly more nontraditional women, particularly the lawyers, were Jewish. This research points to the old stereotype that something in a Jewish background facilitates people (women) becoming nontraditional professionals (particularly doctors and lawyers). Perhaps the surprising finding is that only 10% of the doctors were Jewish (30% of the lawyers were Jewish). The differences discussed pertaining to sources of financial support deserve similar attention. Is there anything about parents working or loans as sources of aid that influenced these women? Similarly, what is it about participating in organizations that effects women's career plans? Do early interests in reading as opposed to participation in domestic activities affect women's career development? At present, the data are too limited to answer these questions or conclude which variables definitely influence women's career development.

Implications for Women's Career Development and Future Research

Although the data cannot answer all of the questions raised, the study does pave the way for future research both in terms of the variables to be tested and the methods to be used. Specific variables such as presence or absence of role models need to be investigated. For example, research exploring the effects of career choice of young girls exposed to single professional women and married professional women in traditional and nontraditional fields should be encouraged. These models could be presented as book or t.v. personalities or by field trips to observe employed women in various fields. In addition to research on the effects of role models, research investigating how to encourage various career choices should be carried out. Questions such as—What kind of encouragement is perceived as helpful/harmful? By whom? In what context? For what?—need to be addressed. At present, though, one would predict that the presence of these powerful and nurturant role models combined with sources of encouragement enhance career development.

The findings that nontraditional women are not "deviants" from traditional female role stereotypes except in their present career status and that they are, in fact, at least as committed and satisfied with their present lives (which includes family and career) as other women needs further exploration before conclusions can be made. Even though contradictions exist between behaviors expected for the instrumental professional role and the expressive role for women, and past research suggests that professional women are treated as deviants, the nontraditional women studied do not appear to perceive themselves as different from other women. Perhaps future research needs to ask these women more directly about their perceptions of their roles as Professional Women, how they perceive themselves in terms of their colleagues and peers. In addition, colleagues, family and close friends of professional women as well as consumers of professional women's services need to be questioned about their perceptions and reactions to professional women. To explain this lack of difference, one could speculate that the results of past laboratory studies largely based on college populations cannot be generalized to people in general; or, these women are unaware of the negative reactions they have received; or, the questions asked in the present study were not capable of drawing out these differences. Studies comparing these high status nontraditional women with women executives in high status nonemployment positions such as executives in the League of Women Voters or board members in social welfare organizations, should be implemented in order to compare the effects of salaries on perceptions of women who assume instrumental roles. At present, the research suggests that the presence of a nontraditional career does not predict a nontraditional background nor a nonconforming present lifestyle.

The following variables generated by the present study as well as by past studies also warrant further investigation in terms of their predictability on women's career development: the quantity and type of reactions to previous job experiences, participation in and reactions to women's support groups, societal issues, grades, participation in organizations, sources of and reactions to financial support, mother's and father's employment history, mother's and father's educational background, family constellation, daughter-parent relationship, religious background, marital and family status, commitment and reactions to present life/career situation, and self-perceptions characteristics. At present although they have all shown to have some relationship to women's nontraditional career development, results about their influence are limited, sometimes contradictory and therefore inconclusive.

The issue relating to attitudes also warrants further research. Although the presence of the above variables may in fact positively affect women's career development, this research suggests, however, that it is not merely the presence of a variable but the reactions to the variable which affects career development. Thus, questions in future research which relate to a variable must also address what influence, if any, the presence or absence of a variable has had on the woman's career development. In other words, instead of making assumptions about a variable's importance, women should be asked directly. If research continues to support the importance of a positive self-image for career development, then future research must address how these nontraditional women learned to feel positively about themselves. For example, was it an innate quality they recognized? Or did their parents or teachers foster this positive self-image? In addition, if research continues to suggest that women in nontraditional professions feel more satisfied and committed to their present lives than other groups of women then research must continue to explore this issue. What is it about their lives that made nontraditional women more satisfied than homemakers?

The data collected in this study primarily discussed what variables women feel have helped maintain their career decisions. Questions specifically addressing women's original career choices need to be developed and tested.

Besides modifying old questions or developing new questions which address the above variables, several other methodological issues were raised in this study. For example, research on men in these same occupations should be explored and compared to the women studied. The retrospective technique used in this study may be largely responsible for the present findings, which differ from past research studies. Problems also exist with retrospective studies. For example, asking subjects to respond to issues relating to their childhood or even a few years before can lead to distortions in memory and therefore biased responses. However, since the three different methods of collecting the data, questionnaire, mini-phone interview and face-to-face interview, largely yielded parallel results, one would speculate that the results obtained from the retrospective studies are more valid than those from expectation studies. Thus, the data suggests that retrospective techniques with women who have actually become professionals should be continued. The women should be from various professional fields in various parts of the country and should be grouped in their specific professional field as well as in their nontraditional, traditional or homemaking category. Longitudinal studies investigating career development throughout women's lives should also be encouraged.

Qualitative data from the open-ended questions provided some new information as well as information which seems better able to distinguish the various groups of women. Although the analysis of these subjective responses is more difficult and less interpretable than the quantifiable objective data, the qualitative information they provide warrant their inclusion in future studies.

Conclusion

This study provides clear evidence of substantial differences among the five groups of women. The most salient difference seems to reflect the presence of nontraditional supportive role models throughout the lives of the doctors and lawyers. In some ways, however, more similarities than differences in the women's backgrounds were found. This study concludes that women who assume nontraditional career statuses do not necessarily experience atypical backgrounds or lead nonconforming lives and should not be treated as "deviants" from normative behaviors expected of women. In addition, the study raises many issues relating to women's career development which lend themselves to future research.

Limitations, Strengths and Suggested Modifications

Several limitations and strengths of the present study should be noted. First, and most important, the women in the samples are not necessarily representative of the women in their fields, and are certainly not representative of women in the United States. The doctors sampled were members of the American Medical Women's Association, the home economists members of their state Home Economics Association, and the nurses were limited to public health nurses. The Colorado homemakers were chosen because they were either wives of a "professional" and/or wives of a "faculty" and the Ohio homemakers were members of the women's faculty club. Not only were these homemakers not representative of all "homemakers" because of their husband's high socioeconomic status, but some of the returned questionnaires were from women who were not even homemakers. Eighteen of these women's questionnaires had to be excluded from the study because four were answered by the teenage daughter instead of the wives in the household and 14 were sufficiently employed so as to not be considered homemakers as defined in this study. It is impossible to assess how many other "nonhomemakers" were sent questionnaires.

Despite the limitations of the sampling method, the large sample of women were randomly selected from a variety of professions (including homemaking) in two states. Therefore, the sample probably more accurately represents professional women than most of the samples in the research literature since most samples are drawn from a single major at one school or from a single profession at best. In addition, this study's sample reflects women who are actually practicing in their respective professions, and therefore reflects actual rather than potential career choice.

Further, although the response rate for the mailed questionnaire was only 48%, the interview response rate was 92% and the mini-questionnaire response rate was 89%. Including all of these subjects, the overall response rate was 59%. For those studies which even report their response rate, 59% is well within the range reported. One possible explanation as to why the response rate was so high could be the relevance of the contents of the cover letter and the questionnaire to these women. Besides being personally addressed to each woman, the cover letter detailed the rationale and goals of the study as well as offered the option to receive a copy of the results. Not only did almost every woman responding request a copy of the results, but several wrote letters thanking the author for letting them participate in this study. They found the questionnaire extremely thought provoking and were anxious to see how they compared with other women. Also unexpected, were the apologetic letters received from women explaining why they could not participate. One woman did respond, however, that she felt the questionnaire was meaningless and not worth her time.

The results in this study demonstrate that for the most part the three methods of investigation obtained similar findings. Differences which arose because of the type of instrument used, questionnaire, mini-phone interview, or long face-to-face interview, were rare and seemed unimportant to the finding. Therefore, the data suggests that the responders are representative of the samples they were chosen from. Other studies do not account for this additional potential source of responder/nonresponder bias (Lemkau, 1979). In addition, the mini-phone questionnaire procedure elicited some other valuable information. Several of these women, particularly the lawyers, reported having never received a mailed questionnaire. They said they had moved and the questionnaire had not reached them at their new address. There is no way of assessing how many of the "nonresponders" fell into this category. Future researchers may opt to use first class rather than bulk mailing in their studies in order to better assess their actual response rate.

Another problem concerns the biases inherent in all self-report studies, particularly when the subject is asked to respond about childhood memories. In this study, however, this bias exists across all five groups of women and is not likely to affect any one group more than any other. Thus, the chances of one professional group being described in an extreme manner because of the subject's self-reporting are minimized because all of the groups being tested reflect this same problem. In addition, the results demonstrating that the three methods of investigation yielded similar findings suggests that the presence or absence of another person did not cause the subjects to self-report differently; i.e., the women were neither encouraged nor discouraged to color their background.

The instrument used also had some problems which were not discovered until the interview sessions, or even as late as when the coding manual was being developed. For example, blank responses to the more open-ended questions such as "employment during high school" could be interpreted to mean a number of things such as: none at all, no jobs worthy of listing, or the subject felt the question was not worth responding to. Future researchers would need to refine this type of question to insure consistent answers (e.g., lists of numbers, 0–1, 2–3, 4–5, could be provided along with lists of the types of jobs, waitress, mechanic, babysitter, other). Other questions such as "hobbies" or "reasons for leaving your job" had similar limitations. Questions such as "How long did it take you to earn this degree?" or "Before completing this degree, had you ever discontinued your education for a period of time?" did not have clear reference points and subsequently resulted in inconsistent findings. More specific questions such as "How old were you when you received your high school diploma, college degree, masters, Ph.D., J.D., M.D., etc.?" or "Before completing your college degree, had you ever discontinued your education?" would result in more meaningful and consistent data.

Part III, the open-ended portion of the questionnaire presented problems in analysis. Although most women responded in a few paragraphs, some women wrote pages of answers while others wrote a sentence or nothing at all. Because of the variety in type and quantity of responses, the data did not lend itself to systematic statistical analysis. For exploratory questions, however, these open-ended questions were quite valuable. The responses did elaborate on some of the information concerning previous variables suggested as well as elicit some new variables which pioneer women support as having positively affected their professional development. These questions also afforded the opportunity for several women to report "regrets" they have with their present life situations. Therefore, these open-ended questions served their purpose and paved the way for future research.

Despite these problems, the questionnaire developed for this study incorporated several refinements from previous studies in the questions posed. For example, the questions concerned with parents' occupational background asked specifics about the mother's and father's employment history throughout the subject's life. Previous studies merely asked if the subject's parent was presently working or had ever worked and did not reflect the parent's working habits, both the type and times of employment. The present study suggested that the mother's employment does change and the various work periods need to be tested and analyzed separately. Thus, the need for more detailed questions in further research is suggested by the study.

Appendix A

QUESTIONNAIRE

BACKGROUND INVENTORY

EMPLOYMENT BACKGROUND

Present employment position: _____

Present employer: _____

Time employed with this employer: Years _____ Months _____

PAST JOBS

                    Position/Employer   Dates Employed   Reason for Leaving

Most Recent

Employment during
High School

GENERAL BACKGROUND

Highest degree attained: _____

When did you receive this? _____

How old were you when you received this? _____

How long did it take you to earn this degree? _____

Where did you earn this degree? _____

Before completing this degree, had you every discontinued your
education for a period of time? _____

If yes, for how long? _____

Why? _____

Age: _____ Height: _____ Weight: _____ Race: _____

Ethnic group or nationality: _____

High School Grade Point Average: _____ College Grade Point Average: _____

Post–College Grade Point Average (e.g., medical school): _____

College Major: _____

How did you finance your education: _____

Mother's Age: _____ (If deceased, when 19___ age ____)

Father's Age: _____ (If deceased, when 19___ age ____)

Parents' Marital Status:

    Married and living together _____

    Divorced or separated _____ How long? _____

Mother's/Father's (M/F) Occupation:

    Before you were 5 years old: M: Position: _____
                                Years Employed: _____ Days/Week _____

                                  F: Position: _____
                                  Years Employed: _____ Days/Week _____

    When you were 5 yrs–18 yrs: M: Position: _____
                                  Years Employed: _____ Days/Week _____

                                  F: Position: _____
                                  Years Employed: _____ Days/Week _____

    When you were 18–present: M: Position: _____
                                  Years Employed: _____ Days/Week _____

                                  F Position: _____
                                  Years Employed: _____ Days/Week _____

Parents' Educational Attainment: Mother_____ Father _____

Birth order—write out your family constellation,
  e.g., 1. older brother (33 yrs.)
      2. older brother (32 yrs.)
      3. myself (26 yrs.)

_____ (oldest child)

_____

_____

_____

_____ (youngest child)

Did anyone else live with your family when you were growing up? _____

If yes, tell the relationship and the years the person lived with you:

_____

Religious upbringing: Agnostic   Atheist   Catholic   Jewish   Protestant
                        Unitarian   Other _____

Places lived: (city, state and type of dwelling (e.g., Phila., Pa.,
                                                    private house)

   as a child: _____

   during college: _____

   after college: _____

   presently: _____

Hobbies as a child: _____

Age of first date: _____

Organizations were member of: Leadership Positions:

   High School _____   _____

   College _____   _____

   Post-College School _____   _____

   Presently _____   _____

Marital Status: _____

   If married, for how long? _____

   If divorced, separated, or widowed, for how long? _____

      How long were you married? _____

   Number of children: _____   Children's ages: _____

   If not married, are you living with anyone (e.g., parents, roommates,

      lover)? _____ Relationship _____

   While you were in college, were you married? _____

   If no, did you have any close supportive relationships? _____

      sex of person(s) _____

While you were in post-college training, were you married? _____

If no, did you have any close supportive relationships? _____

    sex of person(s) _____

Which of the following best describes your present situation?
(Circle a numbered response and the correct item on the scale following your response.)

If <u>unmarried</u> (includes single, separated, divorced or widowed)

1. I anticipate remaining unmarried and childless, pursue employment only.

2. I anticipate remaining unmarried while combining childrearing with (part-time, full-time) employment.

3. I anticipate remaining employed and childless while also getting married.

4. I anticipate remaining employed only until marriage.

5. I anticipate remaining employed only before children are born, then becoming a full-time homemaker.

6. I anticipate remaining employed before children are born, then resuming (part-time, full-time) employment after my youngest child is _____.

7. I anticipate resuming (part-time, full-time) employment after my youngest child is _____.

Commitment to this choice:

1	2	3	4	5
very weak	somewhat weak	average	somewhat strong	very strong

If <u>married without children</u>:

8. I anticipate remaining childless and continuing employment.

9. I anticipate remaining employed only before children are born, then becoming a full-time homemaker.

10. I anticipate remaining employed before children are born, then resuming (part-time, full-time) employment after my youngest child is _____.

11. I anticipate always combining marriage and child-rearing with (part-time, full-time) employment.

Commitment to this choice:

1	2	3	4	5
very weak	somewhat weak	average	somewhat strong	very strong

If married with children:

12. I am a full-time homemaker and anticipate remaining a full-time homemaker.

13. I anticipate resuming employment after my youngest child is _____.

14. I am combining marriage and childrearing with (part-time, full-time) employment.

Commitment to this choice:

1	2	3	4	5
very weak	somewhat weak	average	somewhat strong	very strong

The people who are presently closest to me are:

(sex) _____ (age) _____ (relationship) _____

(sex) _____ (age) _____ (relationship) _____

My present hobbies are: _____

The farthest distance I have ever travelled is _____

How old were you: _____ Did you travel alone: _____

If no, with whom did you travel: _____

CIRCLE THE NUMBER WHICH BEST DESCRIBES YOU:

How tall do you perceive yourself compared with other women you know who are around your age?

1	2	3	4	5
shorter than almost all (90%)	shorter than 75%	average	taller than 75%	taller than almost all (90%)

How physically strong do you perceive yourself compared with other women you know who are around your age?

1	2	3	4	5
weaker than 90%	weaker than 75%	average	stronger than 75%	stronger than 90%

How physically attractive do you perceive yourself compared with other women you know who are around your age?

1	2	3	4	5
less attractive than almost all (90%)	less attractive than 75%	average	more attractive than 75%	more attractive than almost all (90%)

How intelligent do you perceive yourself compared with other women you know who are around your age?

1	2	3	4	5
less intelligent than almost all (90%)	less intelligent than 75%	average	more intelligent than 75%	more intelligent than almost all (90%)

How self-confident do you perceive yourself compared with other women you know who are around your age?

1	2	3	4	5
less self-confident than almost all (90%)	less self-confident than 75%	average	more self-confident than 75%	more self-confident than almost all (90%)

If your mother was employed since you were born, please answer:

What effect do you think your mother's employment had on your career development?

1	2	3	4	5
very negative influence	some negative influence	none	some positive influence	very positive influence

If your mother was never employed since you were born, please answer:

What effect do you think your mother's nonemployment had on your career development?

1	2	3	4	5
very negative influence	some negative influence	none	some positive influence	very positive influence

My relationship with my mother is: (if no longer alive, my relationship with my mother during the last two years before her death was:)

1	2	3	4	5
very hostile	somewhat hostile	indifferent	somewhat warm/ caring	very warm/ caring

My relationship with my father is: (if no longer alive, my relationship with my father during the last two years before her death was:)

1	2	3	4	5
very hostile	somewhat hostile	indifferent	somewhat warm/ caring	very warm/ caring

My relationship with my mother when I was a young child was:

1	2	3	4	5
very hostile	somewhat hostile	indifferent	somewhat warm/ caring	very warm/ caring

My relationship with my father when I was a young child was:

1	2	3	4	5
very hostile	somewhat hostile	indifferent	somewhat warm/ caring	very warm/ caring

As a child, I recall doing what my parents told me:

1	2	3	4	5
less than 10% of the time	less than 25% of the time	50% of the time	more than 75% of the time	more than 90% of the time

As a child, I recall being friendly and outgoing:

1	2	3	4	5
less than 10% of the time	less than 25% of the time	50% of the time	more than 75% of the time	more than 90% of the time

As a child, I recall being independent:

1	2	3	4	5
less than 10% of the time	less than 25% of the time	50% of the time	more than 75% of the time	more than 90% of the time

As a child, I recall being assertive:

1	2	3	4	5
less than 10% of the time	less than 25% of the time	50% of the time	more than 75% of the time	more than 90% of the time

As a child, I recall being competitive:

1	2	3	4	5
less than 10% of the time	less than 25% of the time	50% of the time	more than 75% of the time	more than 90% of the time

As a child, I recall unhappy experiences:

1	2	3	4	5
less than 10% of the time	less than 25% of the time	50% of the time	more than 75% of the time	more than 90% of the time

As a child, I recall being self-confident:

1	2	3	4	5
less self-confident than almost all (90%)	less self-confident than 75%	average	more self-confident than 75%	more self-confident than almost all (90%)

As a child, I was:

1	2	3	4	5
always a "tomboy"	usually a "tomboy"	50/50 combination	usually feminine	always feminine

As a child, I played with:

1	2	3	4	5
all boys	mostly boys	about equally boys and girls	mostly girls	all girls

During my high school years, I regularly kept company with:

1	2	3	4	5
no one	1 or 2 people about my age	3 or 4 people about my age	5 or 6 people about my age	7 or more people about my age

During my high school years, my interests and commitment to a career in which women often enter (e.g., nursing, teaching) were:

1	2	3	4	5
very weak	somewhat weak	average	somewhat strong	very strong

During my high school years, my interests and commitment to a career in which women do not often enter (e.g., medicine, law) were:

1	2	3	4	5
very weak	somewhat weak	average	somewhat strong	very strong

During my college years, my interests and commitment to a career in which women often enter (e.g., nursing, teaching) were:

1	2	3	4	5
very weak	somewhat weak	average	somewhat strong	very strong

During my college years, my interests and commitment to a career in which women do not often enter (e.g., medicine, law) were:

1	2	3	4	5
very weak	somewhat weak	average	somewhat strong	very strong

During adolescence my thoughts and commitment to getting married were:

1	2	3	4	5
very weak	somewhat weak	average	somewhat strong	very strong

During adolescence my thoughts and commitment to raising children were:

1	2	3	4	5
very weak	somewhat weak	average	somewhat strong	very strong

During college, my thoughts and commitment to getting married were:

1	2	3	4	5
very weak	somewhat weak	average	somewhat strong	very strong

During college my thoughts and commitment to raising children were:

1	2	3	4	5
very weak	somewhat weak	average	somewhat strong	very strong

My employment history (the type and quantity of jobs I've experienced) happened:

1	2	3	4	5
completely by chance	mostly by chance	equally by chance and planning	mostly by planning	completely by planning

What effect do you think your employment history had on your career/noncareer development?

very negative influence	some negative influence	none	some positive influence	very positive influence

Please explain your last two answers concerning your employment history.

If you changed your career plans, please explain what led you to this decision.

Was there any significant person(s) in your life whom you feel either positively or negatively influenced your career/noncareer development?

Please explain (i.e., who influenced you and how).

Was there any significant experience(s) in your life which you feel either positively or negatively influenced your choice of career or non-career?

Please explain.

Check any of the following women's groups you have been a member of and your level of participation:

Group	Participation/Commitment		
	1	2	3
	Infrequent/casual	average	frequent/strong
_____Professional Women's Organization	1	2	3
_____Consciousness Raising Group	1	2	3
_____Volunteer Service Group	1	2	3
_____Women's Social Group	1	2	3
_____League of Women's Voters	1	2	3
_____Women's Religious Group	1	2	3
_____Auxilliary Group (e.g., American Legion, any group associated with husband's job--Faculty wives)	1	2	3
_____Moderate Feminist Group (e.g., N.O.W.)	1	2	3
_____Women's Political Group	1	2	3
_____Other--Specify	1	2	3

If you checked any of the above, what effects do you feel this experience had on your career development?

1	2	3	4	5
very negative influence	some negative influence	none	some positive influence	very positive influence

If you did not check any of the groups, do you think you would like to join one? _____

If yes, which type? _____ Why?

The following section could be the most valuable part of the questionnaire. Please take some time now to consider your life and, specifically, your career development. Are there any critical factors in your life which you feel have influenced your career development (for example, something within you, your employment background, important relationships, hobbies, particular events, particular individuals, or anything else)? If there is more than one factor, please list each and describe briefly.

Appendix B

The Ohio State University   **Department of Psychology**

164 West Nineteenth Avenue
Columbus, Ohio 43210

Phone 614 422-6649

August, 1977

Dear

    This questionnaire is a part of my doctoral research investigating factors which women feel have been important in their career development. Hopefully, the information gathered from you will enable counselors, teachers, social change agents and other women to better understand the factors affecting women's life/career choices, the support women receive, the problems women face and the kind of changes that could make present environments more supportive of women choosing a variety of careers.

    You have been selected to participate in this study because of your given career in medicine, home economics, nursing, law or homemaking. I would like to invite you to participate in this study, with the understanding that ALL THE INFORMATION I COLLECT WILL BE TREATED IN STRICT CONFIDENCE. Because your name has been randomly selected and because the information you have may be very valuable for this research and other women, I would greatly appreciate your cooperation in filling out the questionnaire.

    The questionnaire will take about 15-30 minutes of your time, and may require some reflection and thought. I realize that this may be a sizeable intrusion in a busy time schedule, but I hope you agree that the goals of the study are sufficiently important to justify your effort. Please return your completed questionnaire within the next two weeks in the enclosed stamped envelope. When you return the questionnaire, the coding information used will be destroyed. The coding is being used for mailing purposes only to insure you that your responses will remain anonymous while also enabling me to know who has returned a questionnaire.

    On the questions themselves, there are, of course, no 'right answers' other than your opinion. YOUR ANSWERS WILL BE ANONYMOUS--PLEASE ANSWER AS CANDIDLY AS POSSIBLE. If you find particular questions unclear or confusing, please feel free to clarify your answers with a note.

    If you would like more information about the study, feel free to write or call me at the Clinical Psychology Department address above. If you are interested in receiving the results, please let me know this on a slip of paper or the questionnaire. I will be happy to send a summary of the study to you.

    I would like to thank you in advance for your cooperation in helping me and other women.

Sincerely yours,

Jill ann Steinberg

Jill Ann Steinberg

College of Social and Behavioral Sciences

Appendix C

MINI - QUESTIONNAIRE

BACKGROUND INVENTORY

EMPLOYMENT BACKGROUND

Present employment position: _____

Present employer: _____

Time employed with this employer: Years _____ Months _____

PAST JOBS

             Position/Employer   Dates Employed   Reason for Leaving

Most Recent

Employment during
High School

GENERAL BACKGROUND

Highest degree attained: _____

  When did you receive this? _____

  How old were you when you received this? _____

  How long did it take you to earn this degree? _____

  Where did you earn this degree? _____

  Before completing this degree, had you every discontinued your
  education for a period of time? _____

  If yes, for how long? _____

  Why? _____

Age: _____   Height: _____   Weight: _____   Race: _____

Ethnic group or nationality: _____

High School Grade Point Average: _____   College Grade Point Average: _____

Post—College Grade Point Average (e.g., medical school): _____

College Major: _____

How did you finance your education: _____

Mother's Age: _____ (If deceased, when 19___ age ____)

Father's Age: _____ (If deceased, when 19___ age ____)

Parents' Marital Status:

    Married and living together _____

    Divorced or separated _____   How long? _____

Mother's/Father's (M/F) Occupation:

    Before you were 5 years old: M: Position: _____
                                 Years Employed: _____ Days/Week _____

                               F: Position: _____
                                 Years Employed: _____ Days/Week _____

    When you were 5 yrs-18 yrs: M: Position: _____
                                 Years Employed: _____ Days/Week _____

                                 F: Position: _____
                                 Years Employed: _____ Days/Week _____

    When you were 18—present: M: Position: _____
                                 Years Employed: _____ Days/Week _____

                                 F Position: _____
                                 Years Employed: _____ Days/Week _____

Parents' Educational Attainment: Mother_____   Father _____

Birth order--write out your family constellation,
  e.g., 1. older brother (33 yrs.)
       2. older brother (32 yrs.)
       3. myself (26 yrs.)

_____ (oldest child)

_____

_____

_____

_____ (youngest child)

Did anyone else live with your family when you were growing up? _____

If yes, tell the relationship and the years the person lived with you:

_____

Religious upbringing: Agnostic   Atheist   Catholic   Jewish   Protestant
                      Unitarian   Other _____

Marital Status: _____

   If married, for how long? _____

   If divorced, separated, or widowed, for how long? _____

      How long were you married? _____

   Number of children: _____ Children's ages: _____

   If not married, are you living with anyone (e.g., parents, roommates,

   lover)? _____ Relationship _____

While you were in post-college training, were you married? _____

   If no, did you have any close supportive relationships? _____

      sex of person(s) _____

Which of the following best describes your present situation?
(Circle a numbered response and the correct item on the scale following
your response.)

   If <u>unmarried</u> (includes single, separated, divorced or widowed)

      1. I anticipate remaining unmarried and childless, pursue employment
         only.

      2. I anticipate remaining unmarried while combining childrearing with
         (part-time, full-time) employment.

      3. I anticipate remaining employed and childless while also getting
         married.

      4. I anticipate remaining employed only until marriage.

      5. I anticipate remaining employed only before children are born, then
         becoming a full-time homemaker.

      6. I anticipate remaining employed before children are born, then
         resuming (part-time, full-time) employment after my youngest child
         is _____.

      7. I anticipate resuming (part-time, full-time) employment after my
         youngest child is _____.

Commitment to this choice:

1	2	3	4	5
very weak	somewhat weak	average	somewhat strong	very strong

If <u>married without children</u>:

8. I anticipate remaining childless and continuing employment.

9. I anticipate remaining employed only before children are born, then becoming a full-time homemaker.

10. I anticipate remaining employed before children are born, then resuming (part-time, full-time) employment after my youngest child is _____.

11. I anticipate always combining marriage and child-rearing with (part-time, full-time) employment.

Commitment to this choice:

1	2	3	4	5
very weak	somewhat weak	average	somewhat strong	very strong

If <u>married with children</u>:

12. I am a full-time homemaker and anticipate remaining a full-time homemaker.

13. I anticipate resuming employment after my youngest child is _____.

14. I am combining marriage and childrearing with (part-time, full-time) employment.

Commitment to this choice:

1	2	3	4	5
very weak	somewhat weak	average	somewhat strong	very strong

Check any of the following women's groups you have been a member of and your level of participation:

Group	Participation/Commitment		
	1 Infrequent/casual	2 average	3 frequent/strong
____Professional Women's Organization	1	2	3
____Consciousness Raising Group	1	2	3
____Volunteer Service Group	1	2	3
____Women's Social Group	1	2	3
____League of Women's Voters	1	2	3
____Women's Religious Group	1	2	3
____Auxilliary Group (e.g., American Legion, any group associated with husband's job--Faculty wives)	1	2	3
____Moderate Feminist Group (e.g., N.O.W.)	1	2	3
____Women's Political Group	1	2	3
____Other--Specify	1	2	3

If you checked any of the above, what effects do you feel this experience had on your career development?

1	2	3	4	5
very negative influence	some negative influence	none	some positive influence	very positive influence

If you did not check any of the groups, do you think you would like to join one? _____

If yes, which type? _____ Why?

The following section could be the most valuable part of the questionnaire. Please take some time now to consider your life and, specifically, your career development. Are there any critical factors in your life which you feel have influenced your career development (for example, something within you, your employment background, important relationships, hobbies, particular events, particular individuals, or anything else)? If there is more than one factor, please list each and describe briefly.

Appendix D

BACKGROUND INVENTORY CODE

Card #	Column #	Question #	Variable	Code (Rows)
1	1,2,3		Subject's number	- - -
1	4		Card #	1 = Card #1
1	5		Type of Response	1 = Returned questionnaire 2 = Face-to-Face interview 3 = Mini-phone interview
1	6	1	Present "employment" position	1 = Home economist 2 = Doctor 3 = Lawyer 4 = Homemaker 5 = Nurse 6 = Misc./homemaker--professional
1	7,8	3	Time employed with this employer (years)	- - years
1	9,10	3	Time employed with this employer (months)	- - months 99 = N/A (presently unemployed, includes homemaker, retired)
1	11	4A	# Jobs after high school	0 = none 1 = 1 job (present job) 2 = 2 jobs (present 1 plus 1) 8 > 8 jobs (present 1 plus 7)

Card #	Column #	Question #	Variable	Code (Rows)
1	12	4B	# Fields jobs were in	1 = same as present field 2 = same field plus 1 more field 6 = same field plus $\geq$ 5 more fields 7 = can not determine 9 = N/A (none on previous answer)
1	13	4C	Jobs in high school	0 = none 1 = 1 job 7 = $\geq$ jobs
REASONS FOR LEAVING JOB				
1	14	4D	moved	1 = No 2 = Yes 9 = N/A (still employed, never left a job)
1	15	4D	More desirable position (advancement, better pay, etc.)	Same as above
1	16	4D	Finished degree	Same as above
1	17	4D	Position in conjunction with earning a degree (e.g., teaching associate, internship)	Same as above
1	18	4D	Marriage	Same as above
1	19	4D	Children, pregnancy, family responsibility	Same as above
1	20	4D	Husband changed job/husband's education	Same as above

Card #	Column #	Question #	Variable	Code (Rows)
1	21	4D	More school/advanced training	Same as above
1	22	4D	seasonal or temporary job	Same as above
1	23	4D	Fired	Same as above
1	24	4D	Dissatisfaction with job (needed a change, felt discrimination)	Same as above
1	25	4D	Retired	Same as above
1	26	4D	Health	Same as above
1	27	4D	Travel	Same as above
1	28	4D	Too many jobs	Same as above
1	29	4D	Position terminated/job completed	Same as above
1	30	4D	"Other"—e.g., political reasons, extended vacation, needed time to study	Same as above
1	31	5A	Highest degree attained	1 = high school/some college (business college)
				2 = college/bachelors (and RN)
				3 = masters
				4 = Ph.D.
				5 = J.D.
				6 = M.D.
				7 = M.D. and Ph.D.
				8 = J.D. and Ph.D.
				9 = M.D. and J.D.

Card #	Column #	Question #	Variable	Code (Rows)
1	32,33	5B	# years since received degree	– – (00 = less than one year)
1	34,35	5C	Age received degree	– – years
1	36	5D	# years took subject to earn degree	0 = less than year
				1 = $1 \leq N < 2$
				2 = $2 \leq N < 3$
				3 = $3 \leq N \leq 4$
				↓
				6 = $N \geq 6$
				7 = cannot determine from subject's response
				8 = N/A (includes only high school with some college)
1	37	5F	Subject discontinued her education	1 = no
				2 = yes
1	38,39	5G	If yes, how long	– – years
				99 = N/A
	REASONS FOR LEAVING SCHOOL			
1	40	5H	Marriage	1 = no
				2 = yes
				9 = N/A
1	41	5H	Pregnant, children, family	same as above
1	42	5H	Work, employment (includes wanted more experience in the field)	same as above
1	43	5H	Not enough money	same as above
1	44	5H	Travel	same as above

Card #	Column #	Question #	Variable	Code (Rows)
1	45	5H	Illness—mental and physical	same as above
1	46	5H	Graduated early from previous degree; needed to wait to start further education	same as above
1	47	5H	Put husband through school/husband establish self/went with husband to navy	same as above
1	48	5H	Decide on career, on program, confused, career change	same as above
1	49	5H	Moved	same as above
1	50	5H	Did not desire further schooling	same as above
1	51	5H	Death or illness of important person	same as above
1	52	5H	"Other" (e.g., waiting for sabbatical leave, WWII, had to leave my country, felt original subject area wasn't respected, experience getting a masters was distasteful)	same as above
1	53, 54	6	Age	—Years
1	55, 56	7	Height	—Inches
1	57, 58, 59	8	Weight	—Pounds
1	60	9	Race/ethnic group/nationality	1 = Caucasian 2 = Black 3 = Chicano, Indian 4 = Foreign born

Card #	Column #	Question #	Variable	Code (Rows)
1	61	10	High school grades	1=A > 90 > 3.8 2=A/B > 88 > 3.3-3.7 3=B 85 2.8-3.2 4=B/C 78 2.3-2.7 5=C 75 1.8-2.2 6=D 65 < 1.8 7=doesn't recall 9=N/A (no grades, etc.)
1	62	11	College grades	same as above
1	63	12	Post-college grades	same as above
			COLLEGE MAJOR	
1	64	13	Hard sciences (biology, chemistry, etc.)	1=no 2=yes 9=N/A
1	65	13	Home economics (food and nutrition, etc.)	same as above
1	66	13	Vocational home economics/vocational education	same as above
1	67	13	English (literature)	same as above
1	68	13	Political science (pre-law)	same as above
1	69	13	Theater arts	same as above
1	70	13	Language	same as above
1	71	13	Education (includes physical education)	same as above

Card #	Column #	Question #	Variable	Code (Rows)
1	72	13	Math	same as above
1	73	13	Music	same as above
1	74	13	History	same as above
1	75	13	Social sciences (social work, sociology, psychology, anthropology)	same as above
1	76	13	Fine arts	same as above
1	77	13	Nursing	same as above
1	78	13	"Other" (e.g., religion, economics, business, philosophy)	same as above
2	1,2,3		Subject's number	- - -
2	4		Card #	2=card #2
2	5	14	Parents/trust fund	1=no 2=yes 3=N/A
2	6	14	Scholarships/fellowship/traineeship/ vocational rehabilitation	same as above
2	7	14	Worked	same as above
2	8	14	Husband (includes alimony, G.I. bill)	same as above
2	9	14	Loan—borrowed (includes government, relatives)	same as above

Card #	Column #	Question #	Variable	Code (Rows)
2	10	14	Savings	same as above
2	11	14	Free university (e.g., City College of NY)	same as above
2	12	14	"Other" (Aunt, sister, sabbatical leave)	same as above
2	13	15	Mother's age	1=died or left when subject was 0-2 years 2=died or left when subject was 3-5 3=died or left when subject was 6-10 4=died or left when subject was 11-15 5=died or left when subject was 16-20 6=died or left when subject was >21; lived through subject's upbringing
2	14	16	Father's age	same as above
2	15	17	Parent's marital status	1=married and living together (presently or until one parent died) 2=divorced or separated when subject was 0-2 3=divorced or separated when subject was 3-5 4=divorced or separated when subject was 6-10 5=divorced or separated when subject was 11-15

Card #	Column #	Question #	Variable	Code (Rows)
				6=divorced or separated when subject was 16-20
				7=divorced or separated when subject was >21

MOTHER'S/FATHER'S OCCUPATION

Card #	Column #	Question #	Variable	Code (Rows)
2	16,17	18-A-1	Mother's occupation: before subject was 5 years old	00=homemaker 01=traditional professional 02=nontraditional professional 03=androgynous profession 04=managers and administrators, except farm 05=salesworkers 06=clerical and kindred workers 07=craftsperson and kindred workers 08=operatives, except transport 09=transport equipment operatives 10=laborers, except farm 11=farmers and farm management 12=farm laborers and farm supervisors 13=service workers, except private household 14=private household workers 15=not known 99=N/A (deceased, too ill, retired)

Card #	Column #	Question #	Variable	Code (Rows)
2	18	18-A-2	Mother's field same as daughter's: before subject was 5 years old	1=no 2=yes 3=N/A
2	19	18-A-3	Mother's occupation same as daughter's: before subject was 5 years old	same as 18-A-2
2	20,21	18-A-4	Mother's occupation: subject was 5-18 yrs.	same as 18-A-1
2	22	18-A-5	Mother's field same as daughter's: subject was 5-18 yrs.	same as 18-A-2
2	23	18-A-6	Mother's occupation same as daughter's: subject was 5-18 yrs.	same as 18-A-2
2	24,25	18-A-7	Mother's occupation: subject was older than 18 yrs.	same as 18-A-1
2	26	18-A-8	Mother's field same as daughter's: subject was older than 18 yrs.	same as 18-A-2
2	27	18-A-9	Mother's occupation same as daughter's: subject was older than 18 yrs.	same as 18-A-2
2	28,29	18-B-1	Father's occupation: before subject was 5 years old	same as 18-A-1
2	30	18-B-2	Father's field same as daughter's: before subject was 5 years	same as 18-A-2
2	31	18-B-3	Father's occupation same as daughter's: before subject was 5 years	same as 18-A-2

Card #	Column #	Question #	Variable	Code (Rows)
2	32,33	18-B-4	Father's occupation: subject was 5-18 yrs	same as 18-A-1
2	34	18-B-5	Father's field same as daughter's: subject was 5-18 yrs.	same as 18-A-2
2	35	18-B-6	Father's occupation same as daughter's: subject was 5-18 yrs.	same as 18-A-2
2	36,37	18-B-7	Father's occupation: subject was older than 18 yrs.	same as 18-A-1
2	38	18-B-8	Father's field same as daughter's: subject was older than 18 yrs.	same as 18-A-2
2	39	18-B-9	Father's occupation same as daughter's: subject was older than 18 yrs.	same as 18-A-2
2	40	19-A	Mother's educational background	0=unknown 1=less than high school degree 2=high school degree 3=some college (teacher's certificate) 4=college degree 5=RN 6=masters 7=Ph.D. 8=M.D., DDS 9=J.D.
2	41	19-B	Father's educational background	same as above

Card #	Column #	Question #	Variable	Code (Rows)
2	42	20	Number of children in subject's family	1=only child 2=subject plus 1 sibling 3=subject plus 2 siblings ↓ 8=at least 8 children 9=cannot determine from sub-ject's response
2	43	21	Subject's birth order	1=first born; includes only child 2=second born ↓ 8=youngest of at least 8 children 9=cannot determine from sub-ject's response
2	44	22	Subject has ——— male siblings	0=none, all female or only child 1=1 brother ↓ 8=at least 8 brothers 9=cannot determine from sub-ject's response
2	45	23	Anyone live with subject's family in her lifetime	1=no 2=yes
			IF SOMEONE LIVED IN FAMILY, TELL RELATIONSHIP	
2	46	24	Relative—adult age (e.g., grandmother, grandfather, aunt)	1=no 2=yes 3=N/A

Card #	Column #	Question #	Variable	Code (Rows)
2	47	24	Relative--child age (e.g., cousin, neice)	same as above
2	48	24	Hired person (e.g., housekeeper, hired hand, nannie)	same as above
2	49	24	Boarder--college students	same as above
2	50	24	Friend--of self, or family	same as above
2	51	24	live-in temporary child (e.g., foster child, exchange student)	same as above
2	52	24	Other (e.g., minister, teacher)	same as above
2	53	25	Religious upbringing	1=Agnostic 2=Atheist 3=Catholic 4=Jewish 5=Protestant 6=Unitarian 7=Other (includes Quaker, Hindu, etc.)

HOBBIES - Past

Card #	Column #	Question #	Variable	Code (Rows)
2	54	27	Sports (includes hiking, biking, swimming, bowling, cards, skating, etc.)	1=no 2=yes
2	55	27	Spectator activities (e.g., movies, t.v., plays, ballet, watching sports)	same as above
2	56	27	Reading	same as above

Card #	Column #	Question #	Variable	Code (Rows)
2	57	27	Writing	same as above
2	58	27	Arts and crafts (e.g., photography, macrame, refinishing furniture)	same as above
2	59	27	Domestic activities (e.g., embroidery, sewing, cooking, knitting, floral arranging, entertaining)	same as above
2	60	27	Collecting things (e.g., stamps, rocks)	same as above
2	61	27	Music—singing, playing instruments	same as above
2	62	27	Dance/drama—performing arts	same as above
2	63	27	Nature activities—animals, gardening, picnics, camping, plants, etc.	same as above
2	64	27	Sciences—math, chemistry	same as above
2	65	27	Politics	same as above
2	66	27	Other (e.g., school activities, languages, church activities, daydreaming)	same as above
2	67	28	Age of first date	0 < 12 years 1=13 years 2=14 years 8=20 years 9 > 21 years

Card #	Column #	Question #	Variable	Code (Rows)
			ORGANIZATIONS/LEADERSHIP POSITIONS	
2	68	29	Number of organizations in high school	0=none 1=1 (not many) 2=2 3=3 (includes response of some, various) 4=4 5= >5 (includes many, numerous, too many) 9=N/A
2	69	30	Number of leadership positions in high school	same as above
2	70	31	Number of organizations in college	same as above
2	71	32	Number of leadership positions in college	same as above
2	72	33	Number of organizations in post-college	same as above
2	73	34	Number of leadership positions in post-college	same as above
2	74	35	Number of organizations presently	same as above
2	75	36	Number of leadership positions presently	same as above
2	76	37	Marital status	1=single 2=married 3=divorced/separated 4=widowed

Card #	Column #	Question #	Variable	Code (Rows)
2	79,80	39	If divorced, separated or widowed, how many years	- - years 99=N/A
3	1,2,3		Subject's number	- - -
3	4		Card number	3=card 3
3	5,6	40	How long were you married	- - years 99=N/A
3	7	41	Number of children	0=none 1=1 ↓ 8= >8
3	8,9	42	Age subject had first child	- - years 99=N/A
3	10,11	43A	Oldest child's age	0=subject is pregnant 1=1 ↓ 99=N/A
3	12,13	43B	Youngest child's age	0=subject is pregnant 1=1 ↓ 99=N/A
3	14	44	If not married, living with anyone	1=no 2=yes 9=N/A

Card #	Column #	Question #	Variable	Code (Rows)
3	15	45	Relationship	1=parents 2=roommates/co-owner of house 3=lover/fiance 4=reitrement home 5=child 6=other (aunt) 9=N/A
3	16	46	While in college, were you married	1=no 2=yes 9=N/A
3	17	47	If no (to #46), any close supportive relationships	1=no 2=yes 9=N/A
3	18	48	Sex of person(s)	1=female 2=male 3=female and male 4=N/A
3	19	49	during post-college training, were you married	1=no 2=yes 9=N/A
3	20	50	If no, any close supportive relationships	1=no 2=yes 9=N/A
3	21	51	Sex of person(s)	1=female 2=male 3=female and male 4=N/A

Card #	Column #	Question #	Variable	Code (Rows)
3	22,23	52	Which of the following best fits your situation	01=01 02=02 .↓ 14=14 99=N/A (e.g., retired--none fit)
3	24	53	Commitment to choice	1=1 ↓ 5=5 9=N/A (no response or 99 given for #52)
3	25	54	Sex of #1 person closest to you	1=female 2=male 3=female and male
3	26	55	Age of #1 person closest to you	1=much younger 2=around same age (within 15 years) 3=much older
3	27	56	Relationship of person #2	1=husband 2=lover/boyfriend/fiance 3=mother/father 4=friend/neighbor/roommate 5=colleague/co-worker/ex-boss 6=children/grandchildren 7=sister/brother 8="in-law"--sister, mother, brother 9=other (e.g., psychiatrist, nephew, aunt)

Card #	Column #	Question #	Variable	Code (Rows)
3	28	57	Sex of #2 person closest to you	same as #54
3	29	58	Age of #2 person closest to you	Same as #55
3	30	59	Relationship of #2 person closest to you	Same as #56
	HOBBIES - Present			
3	31	60	Sports	1=no 2=yes
3	32	60	Spectator activities	same as above
3	33	60	Reading	same as above
3	34	60	Writing	same as above
3	35	60	Arts and crafts	Same as above
3	36	60	Domestic activities	same as above
3	37	60	Collecting things	same as above
3	38	60	Music	same as above
3	39	60	Dance	same as above
3	40	60	Nature activities	same as above
3	41	60	Sciences	same as above
3	42	60	Politics	same as above

Card #	Column #	Question #	Variable	Code (Rows)
3	43	60	Traveling	same as above
3	44	60	Childraising/family/grandmothering	same as above
3	45	60	Community work/organizing/volunteer work/ organizations	same as above
3	46	60	People/friends (care for people)	same as above
3	47	60	Other (e.g., language, eat, garage sales, bible study, smoking dope, attending classes)	same as above
COMPARE YOURSELF WITH OTHER WOMEN				
3	48	61	Tall	1=1 ↓ 5=5 9=N/A
3	49	62	Physically strong	same as above
3	50	63	Physically attractive	same as above
3	51	64	Intelligent	same as above
3	52	65	Self-confident	same as above
3	53	66	Mother's employment	same as above
3	54	67	Mother's nonemployment	same as above
3	55	68	Relationship with mother is	same as above

Card #	Column #	Question #	Variable	Code (Rows)
3	56	69	Relationship with father is	same as above
3	57	70	Relationship with mother as child	same as above
3	58	71	Relationship with father as child	same as above
3	59	72	Child—did what parents told	same as above
3	60	73	Child—friendly and outgoing	same as above
3	61	74	Child—independent	same as above
3	62	75	Child—assertive	same as above
3	63	76	Child—competitive	same as above
3	64	77	Child—unhappy experiences	same as above
3	65	78	Child—self-confident	same as above
3	66	79	Child—was tomboy...feminine	same as above
3	67	80	Child, played with	same as above
3	68	81	High school, kept company with	same as above
3	69	82	High school, interest and commitment to traditional career	same as above
3	70	83	High school, interest and commitment to nontraditional career	same as above
3	71	84	College interest and commitment to traditional career	same as above

Card #	Column #	Question #	Variable	Code (Rows)
3	72	85	College, interest and commitment to nontraditional career	same as above
3	73	86	Adolescence—thoughts of marriage	same as above
3	74	87	Adolescence—thoughts of children	same as above
3	75	88	College—thoughts of marriage	same as above
3	76	89	College—thoughts of children	same as above
3	77	90	Employment history	same as above
3	78	91	Effects of employment history	same as above
4	1,2,3		Subject's number	- - -
4	4		Card number	4=card #4
WOMEN'S GROUPS				
4	5	92	Professional women's groups	0=no 1=1 2=2 3=3 4=checked but no number
4	6	92	Consciousness raising group	same as above
4	7	92	Volunteer service group	same as above
5	8	92	Women's social group	same as above

Card #	Column #	Question #	Variable	Code (Rows)
4	9	92	League of women's voters	same as above
4	10	92	Women's religious group	same as above
4	11	92	Auxiliary group	same as above
4	12	92	Moderate feminist group	same as above
4	13	92	Women's political group	same as above
4	14	92	Other (e.g., LaLeche League, gymnastics)	same as above
4	15	93	Effects of women's groups	1=1 ↓ 5=5 9=N/A

Appendix E

Items Used in Regression Equations

Dependent Variables	Independent Variables
Factor 1 — Positive self-image as a child	Home economist | |Nontraditional women
Factor 2 — Positive orientation towards marriage and children	Doctor | Traditional women |OR|
Factor 3 — Mother's nonemployment	Lawyer | Homemakers
Factor 4 — Nontraditional career orientation	Homemaker
Factor 5 — Participation in volunteer groups	Nurse

Independent Variables (continued):

Home economist │ │Nontraditional women
Doctor │ │Traditional women
│OR│
Lawyer │ │Homemakers
Homemaker │ │
Nurse │ │
- - - - - - - - - - - - - - - - -
No. jobs after high school

Jobs after high school

No. fields jobs were in

Mother—same field as daughter (subject was less than 5 years old)

Mother—same occupation as daughter (subject was less than 5 years old)

Mother—same field as daughter (subject was 5-18 years old)

Mother—same occupation as daughter (subject was 5-18 years old)

Mother—same field as daughter (subject was more than 18 years old)

Dependent Variables (continued):

Factor 6 — Negative relationship with parents

Factor 7 — Political activism

Factor 8 — (Present) positive self-image

Factor 9 — Sex appropriate orientation

Factor 10— Self-discipline and planning

Mother—same occupation as daughter
  (subject was more than 18
  years old)

Father's occupation when subject
was less than 5 years old

Father—same field as daughter
  (subject was less than 5
  years old)

Father—same occupation as daughter (subject was less than
  5 years old)

Father—same field as daughter
  (subject was 5-18 years
  old)

Father—same occupation as daughter (subject was 5-18
  years old)

Father—same field as daughter
  (subject was more than 18
  years old)

Father—same occupation as daughter (subject was more than
  18 years old)

Religion

Age

Marital status

No. children subject has

Subject's age when she had her first
child

High school grades

College grades

How subject financed her education

Appendix F

Responses Given to the Open-Ended Questions

	D = doctors
	L = lawyers
	N = nurses
	HEC = home economists
SIGNIFICANT EXPERIENCES - JOB OR EDUCATION RELATED	H = homemaker

	D	L	N	HEC	H
Previous interests or classes were supportive of career/job	5	8	7	31	17

   Some examples:

   4-H club
   politics
   hobbies
   sports
   theater
   Betty Crocker Award
   honorary
   public speaking
   soloist in high school
   science
   research area
   high school
   workshops in field
   liked being in college better than being
    out of college
   liked college and graduate school

	D	L	N	HEC	H
Previous volunteer work was supportive of my career/job	0	1	2	3	5

   Some examples:

   church work
   leadership positions

	D	L	N	HEC	H
Previous jobs were supportive of my career/job development	10	8	23	19	14

   Some examples:

      took a job for financial reasons, found
        out liked working and continued working
      built subject's self-confidence
      opened subject to various people and
       career opportunities
      met the "right" people
      advancement

	D	L	N	HEC	H
Previous group work encouraged subject's career development	2	1	2	2	3

   Some examples:

      life/career planning workshop
      career day in high school
      assertive training
      counseling
      career counseling, tests

	D	L	N	HEC	H
Characteristics of the job positively influenced subject's career development	10	12	22	7	10

   Some examples:

      likes this type of work/area
      desire to work with others, children
      desire to do tasks
      independence
      responsibility
      aspirations, career and educational desires
      capabilities
      desire to reach own potential
      desire for financial independence
      develop professional goals and values
      desire to help family
      desire to be own boss
      hours mesh with family life (9-5, part-time)
      desire to be in the "limelite," be
       recognized
      importance of material comforts
      skills--outlet for creativity
      challenging
      desire to be needed by others

	D	L	N	HEC	H
Previous jobs were not rewarding enough--encouraged subject to further her education for better positions	9	7	7	9	3

Some examples:

    boring, not challenging
    too limited money and status
    could not effect change
    no social life
    dissatisfied with location

	D	L	N	HEC	H
Previous jobs, experiences, or education discouraged subject's career development	1	1	4	3	9

Some examples:
    limited exposure and choices
      poverty background
      limited explanation of careers in high
        school
    felt discrimination
    "rejected" from area
      as a ninth grader wrote to the Dean of
        Mechanical Engineering--his response was
        for her to go into a "feminine" field
      from a writing conference
      from medical school
    bad experience with employer
    dissappointed with graduate school

	D	L	N	HEC	H
"No Response is Needed"--Subject always wanted to be this	23	12	14	21	23

Some examples:

    jobs were a steady progression towards my
      goal
    took any job to finance my desired educa-
      tional/career goal
    only pursued jobs, no career
    "Fell" into job
    natural progression

	D	L	N	HEC	H
"Family obligations first"—positively influenced subject's career development	5	3	5	10	2

    Some examples:

      husband's death (divorce, illness)
      negative heterosexual relationship
      stayed single, no plans for children—does
        not like to be around kids full-time
      was not satisfied at home full-time
      her "duty" to further family achievement
        and reward her parents
      tried work; kids so much happier, sub-
        ject happier, family better, relieved
        her of her guilt
      kids are in school now
      after 20 years out of school, feels like
        a more serious student now

	D	L	N	HEC	H
"Family obligations first"—negatively influenced subject's (nonhomemaking) career development	6	7	11	6	57

    Some examples:

      satisfied full-time at home
      motherhood first-duty-kiss husband everyday
      I am too involved in volunteer groups
      gets more out of helping husband (hostess)
      single parent; must work can't go back to
        school
      with two small kids and limited income...
      sick, elderly parents, wants to be free to
        help them
      problem of being middle-aged when entering
        law—not assertive and am not accepted
        at my age
      moves because of husband's job
      only something to fall back on

	D	L	N	HEC	H
"Societal issues"/demands supported subject's career plans	10	7	3	4	5

    Some examples:

      Great Depression—showed subject better
        be able to support self, not depend on
        the elements

	D	L	N	HEC	H

need for women doctors in India to help
   women
social issues of the 60's--subject wanted
   to effect change
desire for change
interest in women's movement
   important for women to get education and
     careers
   helped subject become more assertive
changes in the Board of Medicine made her
   eligible to practice
child in Germany of my background was
   pushed towards career training

"Social issues"/demands were not supportive of
subject's career development   8   2   6   5   9

   Some examples:

     job market--took positions which were avail-
       able (e.g., teaching, dietician, nursing),
       not necessarily what I wanted
     subject was not willing to move to another
       area
     stayed with nursing, midwifery, which was
       not acceptable in her state
     women not allowed in Priesthood
     only "acceptable" position for women
       (nursing) in the 40's; felt choice was
       between nursing and teaching
     victim of times--no childcare available
     discrimination against women--subject
       unconsciously accepted lower positions
     courses were not available at her
       university

Financial situation was supportive of career   1   1   1   11   0

   Some examples:

     no problem, had resources
     good planning
     G.I. bill supported
     fellowship--went into field where was money
     boss showed subject how to finance further
       education
     needed to put husband through graduate
       school--kept her out of mother role--and
       she realized her commitment to career

	D	L	N	HEC	H

had to work, her husband couldn't support
   her
sabbatical leave enabled her to earn her
   Ph.D.
always had to earn money through childhood--
   showed subject she likes to work

	D	L	N	HEC	H
Financial situation was not supportive of career plans	0	0	3	1	4

   Some examples:

     could not afford further education
     discrimination, without financial support
       from graduate school

SIGNIFICANT PERSONS

	D	L	N	HEC	H
Relative--Positive Role Model	17	6	12	11	14

   Some examples:

     mother worked and raised a family
     mother went back to work after 55 years
       (because her husband died)
     mother didn't work; close knit family
     husband was more fulfilled
     brother had more fun, didn't have to stay
       home
     uncle
     father

	D	L	N	HEC	H
Relative--Negative Role Model	3	6	2	3	7

   Some examples:

     mother (sister) - unhappy, never reached
               potential
              - too dependent on husband
              - struggled to raise her
                children after husband died
              - worked, didn't seem as
                happy with family life

	D	L	N	HEC	H
Nonrelative, person in subject's field--Positive Role Model	5	4	7	19	10

   Some examples:

      teacher
      doctor
      student nurse
      peer
      professional women were stimulating
      lecturer/panel of career women

	D	L	N	HEC	H
Nonrelative--Negative Role Model	0	0	0	2	3

   Some examples:

      teacher; subject wanted to be better than
      professional women are over-worked
      widows, divorced women without careers

	D	L	N	HEC	H
Relative--Positively supported (emotionally and behaviorally) subject with her career	39	33	26	48	50

   Some examples:

      siblings
      grandparents
      parents (mother) - further your education
                   - immigrants, poor-work
                     hard
                   - parents were interested
                     in my field (politics)
                   - encouraged subject to
                     study not date
                   - got subject into task,
                     not friend, activities
      husband - shared child care
             - asked subject to join him in
               his work
      children - cooperative
             - adopted a "problem" child;
              subject became interested in
              social work

	D	L	N	HEC	H

Relative--discouraged subject's career development

  Some examples:

    parents - "you're too sensitive"
         - women should stay home with the
          children
         - women shouldn't go into man's
          field
         - told subject what to do (get an
          education); she rejected that
         - family without education
    father - critical, nonaccepting--"You'll
         never be any good"
    children - too much work
    husband - won't help with the children
         - held her back

Nonrelative--Positively encouraged subject	37	20	19	45	31

  Some examples:

    former teacher's philosophy--learn
      everything, achieve
    supervisor
    advisor
    professors, chair of department
    Priest
    friends/peers - gave subject a home away
             from home
            - believed in equality of men
             and women
            - in same field, dedicated
    colleagues in field - mentors, boss
    housekeeper
    therapist

Nonrelative--discouraged subject's career development	5	3	4	0	2

  Some examples:

    male colleagues
    boyfriends

	D	L	N	HEC	H

SUBJECT'S CHARACTERISTICS

	D	L	N	HEC	H
Positive characteristics—positively influenced subject's career development	22	10	10	18	8

    Some examples:

        needs stimulation
        bright (Valedictorian)--expected to go on
        intellectual curiosity--ability to plan and
          prepare
        wondered if I could do it
        competitive
        independent
        personal desire--wanted to do something to
          help others
        assertive
        aggressive
        motivated, inner drive
        did well, plodded through
        self confident
        desire for achievement
        good health
        good genetic make-up
        likes to study; likes to learn, work hard,
          "pride in achieving, in being recognized,
          being known as a woman
        compulsive
        outgoing, gets along with people
        temperament--likes to argue, do research,
          influence others
        risk-taker
        independent, risk taker
        creative

	D	L	N	HEC	H
Negative characteristics—negatively influenced subject's career development	1	2	5	2	9

    Some examples:

        just average intelligence (chose nursing
          over medicine)
        lazy
        not competitive
        without motivation, without drive,
          without commitment, no desire to stay in
          school necessary years

	D	L	N	HEC	H

without perseverance (wanted to marry
  anyway)
without confidence
chronic illness, sickly without energy,
  discouraged
couldn't deal with necessary subjects to
  continue with career—especially noted
  science, chemistry, mathematics
insecure
lack of experience
small (size)—dependent

OTHER SIGNIFICANT EXPERIENCES

Religion—supported subject's career development

	D	L	N	HEC	H
Religion—supported subject's career development	5	2	1	2	1

  Some examples:
    (Catholic) values, stability, missionary
      (help others)
    "Religious conversion"—from Bible study
      became a medical missionary)—church
      retreat, felt an influence
    "God"—"I am who I am because of God"

Meditation—positively influenced subject's
career development

	D	L	N	HEC	H
Meditation—positively influenced subject's career development	1	1	0	0	0

  Some examples:

    has increased my self-sufficiency, con-
      fidence, abilities
    Yoga—has increased my ability to meet
      challenges

Books, T.V., Movies—positively influenced
subject's career plans

	D	L	N	HEC	H
Books, T.V., Movies—positively influenced subject's career plans	0	2	3	0	0

  Some examples:

    into mysteries, trials (lawyer)
    Dr. Kildare (nursing)
    feminist literature

College Environment—positive and negative
influencers

	D	L	N	HEC	H
College Environment—positive and negative influencers	2	2	3	2	3

	D	L	N	HEC	H

Some examples:

   women's college--atmosphere, expected
      women to support each other, pursue
      interests
        - women as important
   too much partying, no time for studying

"Sick" person--positive influence	8	0	11	2	5

Some examples:

   wanted to medically help others--father
      died, felt better medical care would
      have helped him
   polio victim, retardate in family; helped
      sick person
   death of friend; subject became more
      introspective and decided needed more
      for self
   self--sick as a young child

Family background--family constellation	3	2	1	3	3

Some examples:

   sibling competition
   third born with no brothers, father's hopes
      for achievement with sons to her
   competitiveness fostered by three older
      sisters
   third of three, subject became dependent
   oldest daughter, her place to go on for
      college
   second of 10, responsibility for younger
      siblings

Traveling--positive support	0	0	2	1	1

Some examples:

   saw different alternatives
   gained self confidence

Social environment--encouraged career develop ment	3	1	0	0	2

Some examples:

   war--family moved a lot

	D	L	N	HEC	H

dated little because I was a fat child--
  got into studying
lived in a small town, was exciting to go
  away to a college

| REGRETS with present life | 2 | 2 | 3 | 0 | 8 |

Some examples:

  lack of women lawyers to start a firm with,
    may have to change fields
  no social life
  sorry she never had children
  chose between nursing or teaching, would
    have liked zoology
  conflict between career or husband's
    happiness
  only pursued jobs, never thought of a
    career
  no women friends to share ideas with
  with two small kids and limited money,
    can't go back to school; some resentment
    only helped husband

Appendix G

Table 32. College Majors by Five Professional Groups

College Major	Home Economists Percent No	Yes	N	Doctors Percent No	Yes	N	Lawyers Percent No	Yes	N	Homemakers Percent No	Yes	N	Nurses Percent No	Yes	N	Total Percent No	Yes	N
Science $X^2(4)=170.30$, $p<.0001$	95%	5%	62	13%	87%	53	98%	2%	46	86%	14%	78	97%	3%	59	79%	21%	298
Home Economics $X^2(4)=170.56$, $p<.0001$	21%	79%	63	100%	0%	52	98%	2%	47	85%	15%	79	100%	0%	59	79%	21%	300
Nursing $X^2(4)=238.29$, $p<.0001$	98%	2%	63	98%	2%	52	100%	0%	47	92%	8%	79	5%	95%	59	79%	21%	300

Table 33. Mother's Occupational Field was the Same as the
Daughter's When the Subject was Less than 5 Years Old by
Five Professional Groups

	Percent		
	No	Yes	Total N
Home Economists	98	2	64
Doctors	95	5	56
Lawyers	96	4	46
Homemakers	16	84	79
Nurses	97	3	58
Total	76	24	303

Note. $X^2(4) = 202.62$, $p < .0001$

Table 34. College Major—Political Science—by Doctors and
Lawyers

	Percent		
	No	Yes	Total N
Doctors	100	0	53
Lawyers	70	30	47
Total	86	14	100

Note. $X^2(1) = 18.36$, $p < .0001$

Bibliography

Adams, John R. Lawrence, Frederick P. & Cook, Sharla J. Analyzing stereotypes of women in the work force. *Sex Roles,* 1979, *Vol 5,* #5, 581-94.

Ahern, N.C. & Scott, E.L. Career outcomes in a matched sample of men and women Ph.D.s: An analytical report. Washington DC: National Academy Press, 1981, 95 pp.

Allport, Gordon W. *Pattern and growth in personality—A psychological interpretation.* New York: Holt, Rinehart & Winston, 1961.

Almquist, Elizabeth M. Attitudes of college men toward working wives. *The Vocational Guidance Quarterly,* Dec. 1974, *23,* #2, 115-21.

Almquist, Elizabeth M., & Angrist, Shirley S. Role model influences on college women's career aspirations. In A. Theodore (Ed.), *The professional woman,* 1971, pp. 301-23.

Anderson, Jane V. Psychological determinants. In R.B. Kundsin (Ed.), *Women and success,* 1974, pp. 200-207.

Angrist, S.A., & Almquist, E.M. *Careers and contingencies.* Cambridge, Mass.: University Press of Cambridge, Mass., 1975.

Astin, Alexander W., & Panos, Robert J. The Educational and Vocational Development of College Students. Washington D.C.: American Council on Education, 1969.

Astin, Helen S. *The woman doctorate in America: Origins, career and family.* New York: Russell Sage Foundation, 1969.

Astin, H.S. Career development of girls during the high school years. *Journal of Counseling Psychology,* 1968, *15,* 536-40. (a)

Astin, H.S. Stability and change in the career plans of ninth grade girls. *Personnel and Guidance Journal,* 1968, *46,* 961-66. (b)

Astin, Helen S. Factors associated with the participation of women doctorates in the labor force. *Personnel and Guidance Journal,* 1967, *46* (3), 240-45.

Astin, Helen S., & Bayer, Alan E. Sex discrimination in academe. *Educational Record,* Spring 1972, 101-18.

Astin, Helen S., Suniewick, Nancy, & Dweck, Susan (Eds.), *Women: A bibliography on their education and careers.* Washington D.C.: Human Service Press, 1971.

Babbie, Earl R. *Survey research methods.* Bellmont, Calif.: Wadsworth Publishing Company, 1973.

Bachtold, Louise M. Personality characteristics of women of distinction. *Psychology of Women Quarterly,* Fall 1976, *1,* 70-79.

Bachtold, Louise M. Women, eminence and career-value relationships. *Journal of Social Psychology,* 1975, *95,* 187-92.

Bandura, Albert. Social learning theory of identificatory processes. In D.A. Goslin (Ed.), *Handbook of socialization theory and research,* 1969, pp. 213-63.

Baruch, Grace. Girls who perceive themselves as competent: Some antecedents and correlates. *Psychology of Women Quaterly,* Fall 1976, *1,* 38-49.

Basow, Susan A. & Howe, Karen Glasse. Role-model influence: Effects of sex and sex-role attitude in college students. *Psychology of Women Quarterly,* Summer 1980, *Vol 4* (4), 558-72.

Beckman, Linda J. & Houser, Betsy Bosak. The more you have, the more you do: The relationship between wife's employment, sex-role attitudes, and household behavior. *Psychology of Women Quarterly,* Winter 1979, *Vol 4* (2), 160-74.

Benenson, Harold B. Family success and sexual equality: The limits of the dual-career family. *Vassar College, Series: ASA,* 1981, *3144,* 29 pp.

Bernard, Jessie. My four revolutions: An autobiographical history of ASA. In J. Huber (Ed.), *Changing women in a changing society,* 1973, pp. 11-30.

Bernard, Jessie. *Women and the public interest: An essay on policy and protest.* Chicago, New York: Aldine, Atherton, 1971.

Bernard, Jessie. *Academic women.* University Park: The Pennsylvania State University Press, 1964.

Best, Fred. Changing sex roles and worklife flexibility. *Psychology of Women Quarterly,* Fall 1981, *Vol 6*(2), 55-71.

Betz, Nancy E. & Hackett, Gail. The relationship of career-related self-efficacy expectations to perceived career options in college women and men. *Journal of Counseling Psychology,* 1981, *Vol 28,* No. 5, 399-410.

Birnbaum, J. Life patterns and self-esteem in gifted family oriented and career committed women. In M.T.S. Mednick, S.S. Tangri, & L.W. Hoffman (Eds.), *Women and achievement.* New York: John Wiley & Sons, 1975.

Blakeney, P., Schottstaedt, M.F. & Sekula, S. Personality characteristics of women entering medical school over a 1-year period. *Journal of Medical Education,* 1982, *57* (Jan), 42-47.

Boring, Phyllis Zatlin. Sex stereotyping in educational guidance. In *Sex Role Stereotyping in the Schools,* National Education Association, 1973, pp. 14-23.

Broverman, Inge K., Vogel, Susan Raymond, Broverman, Donald M., Clarkson, Frank E., & Rosenkrantz, Paul S. Sex-role stereotypes: A current appraisal. *Journal of Social Issues,* 1972, *28, #2,* 59-79.

Brown, Stephen M. Male versus female leaders: A comparison of empirical studies. *Sex Roles,* 1979, *Vol 5,* No 5, 595-611.

Bryson, Rebecca B., Bryson, Jeff B., Licht, Mark H., & Licht, Barbara G. The professional pair-husband and wife psychologist. *American Psychologist,* Jan. 1976, *31, #1,* 10-16.

Burlew, Ann Kathleen. The experiences of black females in traditional and nontraditional professions. *Psychology of Women Quarterly,* 1982, *6* (Spring), 312-26.

Card, J., Steel, L. & Abeles, R. Sex differences in realization of individual potential for achievement. *Journal of Vocational Behavior,* 1980, *17* 1-21.

Carden, Maren Lockwood. *The new feminist movement.* New York: Russell Sage Foundation, 1974.

Carnegie Commission. *Opportunities for women in high education.* Berkeley: McGraw-Hill, 1973.

Cartwright, Lillian Kaufman. Conscious factors entering into decisions of women to study medicine. *Journal of Social Issues,* 1972, *28,, #2,* 201-17.

Chronicle of Higher Education, January 16, 1978, Vol. xv, No. 18, p. 15.

Collier, Helen V. *Counseling women: A guide for therapists.* New York: The Free Press, 1982.

Combs, J.M. & Tolbert, E.L. Vocational role models of college women. *National Association for Women Deans, Administrators and Counselors,* 1980, *44,* 33-38.

Connolly, T., Burks, E., & Rogers, J. *The woman professional in science and engineering: An empirical study of key career decisions.* A Final Technical Report submitted to the National Science Foundation by Georgia Institute of Technology, April, 1976.

Daniels, Arlene K. *A survey of research concerns on women's issues.* (pamphlet) Washington, D.C.: Association of American Colleges, 1975.

Dellas, Marie, Gaier, Eugene L. & Emihovich, Catherine A. Maternal employment and selected behaviors and attitudes of preadolescents and adolescents. *Adolescence*, fall 1979, *14*,, 55, 579-89.

Dunn, Rita, & Dunn, Kenneth. *How to raise independent and professionally successful daughters.* Englewood Cliffs, N.J.: Prentice-Hall, Inc., 1977.

Ellis, A. *Reason and emotion in psychotherapy.* New York: Lyle-Stuart Press, 1962.

Epstein, Cynthia Fuchs (Ed.), *The other half: Roads to woman's equality.* Prentice-Hall, Inc., Englewood Cliffs,, N.J.: A Prentice Book, 1971.

Epstein, Cynthia Fuchs. Women and the professions. In C.F. Epstein (Ed.), *The other half,* 1971a, 122-34.

Epstein, Cynthia Fuchs. *Woman's place.* Berkeley: University of California Press, 1971b.

Epstein, Cynthia Fuchs. Encountering the male establishment: Sex-status limits on women's careers in the professions. In A. Theodore (Ed.), *The professional woman,* 1971c, 52-73.

Erickson, Lee R. Women in engineering: attitudes, motivations and experiences. *Engineering Education,* 1981, *72* (Nov), 180-82.

Erkut, S. & Mokros, J.R. Professors as models and mentors for college students. Working paper No 65, Center for Research on Women, Wellesley College, 1981, 39 pp.

Fakouri, M.E. Relationships of birth order, dogmatism and achievement motivation. *Journal of Individual Psychology,* 1974, *30,* #2, 216-20.

Farmer, Helen S. Career and homemaking plans for high school youth. *Journal of Counseling Psychology,* 1983, *Vol 30,* No. 1, 40-45.

Freeman, Jo. *The politics of women's liberation: A case study of an emerging social movement and its relation to the policy process.* New York: David McKay Co., Inc., 1975.

Freeman, Jo. The origins of the women's liberation movement. In J. Huber (Ed.), *Changing women in a changing society,* 1973, 30-50.

Frieze, Irene H., Parsons, Jacquelynne E., Johnson, Paula B., Ruble, Diane N. & Zellman, Gail L. *Women and sex roles: A social psychological perspectives.* NY, London: WW Norton & Co., 1978.

Garfinkle, S.H. Occupations of women and black workers, 1962-1974. *Monthly Labor Review,* 1975, *98,* 25-34.

Ginzberg, Eli. *Life styles of educated women.* New York: Columbia University Press, 1966.

Goldberg, Philip A. Are women prejudiced against women? *Trans-action,* 1968, *5* (May), 28-30.

Goldberg, A.S. & Shiflett, S. Goals of male and female college students: Do traditional sex differences still exist? *Sex Roles,* 1981, *7*(Dec.) 1213-22.

Gormly, Richard. Birth order, family size, and psychological masculinity-femininity. *Proceedings of the 76th Annual Convention of the American Psychological Association,* 1968, *3,* 165.

Goslin, David (Ed.), *Handbook of socialization theory and research.* Chicago: Russell Sage, Rand McNally & Co., 1969.

Grant, W. Vance & Eiden, Leo J. *Digest of educational statistics 1982,* National Center for Education Statistics, US Dept of Education, Wash DC, 1982.

Gray, Janet Dreyfus. The married professional woman: An examination of her role conflicts and coping strategies. *Psychology of Women Quarterly,* Spring 1983, *Vol 7*(3), 235-43.

Greenglass, E.R. & Devins, R. Factors related to marriage and career plans in unmarried women. *Sex Roles,* 1982, *8*(Jan), 57-71.

Gross, Edward. Plus Ca Cahnge...? The sexual structure of occupations over time. In A. Theodore, *The professional woman,* 1971, pp. 39-51.

Harmon, Lenore. The life and career plans of young adult college women: A follow-up study. *Journal of Counseling Psychology,* 1981 Sep, *Vol 28* (5), 416-27.

Harmon, L.W. Anatomy of career committment in women. *Journal of Counseling Psychology,* 1970, *17,* 77-80.

Hall, R.M. & Sandler, B.R. *Women Winners.* Research report, Project on the status and education of women, Association of American Colleges, Aug 1982, 14pp.

Hawkins, Richard & Tiedeman, Gary. *The creation of deviance—interpersonal and organizational determinants.* Columbus: Charles E. Merrill Publishing Co., 1975.

Heins, Marilyn, Hendricks, Joanne & Matindale, Lois. The importance of extra-family support on career choices of women. *The Personnel and Guidance Journal,* April 1982, *Vol 60,* No. 8, 455-59.

Helson, Ravenna. The changing image of the career woman. *Journal of Social Issues,* 1972, *28* (2), 33-46.

Hennig, Margaret M. Family dynamics and the successful woman executive. In R.B. Kundsin (Ed.), *Women and success,* 1974, pp. 88-93.

Hoffman, Lois Wladis. The professional woman as mother. In R.B. Kundsin (Ed.), *Women and success,* 1974a, pp. 22-28.

Hoffman, Louis Wladis. Early childhood experiences and women's achievement motives. *Journal of Social Issues,* 1972, 187-205.

Hole, Judith & Levine, Ellen. *Rebirth of feminism.* New York: Quadrangle Books, A New York Time Co., 1973.

Holter, Harriet. *Sex roles and social structure.* Oslow, Norway: Universitetsforlaget, 1970.

Hoyt, Donald P. & Kennedy, Carroll, E. Interest and personality correlates of career-motivated and homemaking-oriented college women. *Journal of Counseling Psychology,* 1958, *5* (1), 44-49.

Houseknecht, Sharon K. & Macke, Anne S. Combining marriage and career: The marital adjustment of professional women. *Journal of Marriage and the Family,* Aug. 1981, 651-61.

Huber, Joan (Ed.), *Changing women in a changing society.* Chicago and London: The University of Chicago Press, 1973.

Hymen, S.P. An evaluation of rational-emotive imagery as a component of rational-emotive therapy in the treatment of test anxiety. Unpublished Masters Thesis at the University of Oregon, September, 1977.

Illfelder, Joyce K. Fear of success, sex role attitudes, and career salience and anxiety levels of college women. *Journal of Vocational Behavior,* 1980, *16,* 7-17.

Kaplan, Susan Romer. Motivations of women over 30 for going to medical school. *Journal of Medical Education,* 1981, *56* (Oct), 856-58.

Kaplan, Susan Romer. A feminist Cinderella tale: Women over thirty in graduate and professional schools. *Journal of the National Association for Women Deans, Administrators and Counselors,* 1982, *45* (Spring), 9-15.

Karman, F.J. *Women: Personal and environmental factors in role identification and career choices.* California University, Los Angeles, Center for the Study of Evaluation, 1973, ERIC, ED 084 383.

Keith, Pat M. Sex-role attitudes, family plans, and career orientations: Implications for counseling. *Vocational Guidance Quarterly,* 1981, *29* (March), 244-52.

Kelly, Susan. Changing parent-child relationships: An outcome of mother returning to college. *Family relations,* 1982, *31* (April), 287-94.

Kingdon, M.A. & Sedlacek, W.E. Differences between women who choose traditional and non-traditional careers. Research report No. 1-81, Counseling Center, Univ. of Maryland, 1981, 7pp.

Kirkpatrick, Martha J. A report on a consciousness raising group for women psychiatrists. *Journal of the American Medical Women's Association,* 1975, May, *306,* 206-12.

Knepper, P.R., Elliott, S.A. & Albright, V. Women and minorities in administration of higher education institutions: Employment patterns and salary comparisons 1978-1979 and an analysis of progress toward affirmative action goals 1975-1976 to 1978-1979. *Journal of the College and University Personnel Association,* 1981, *32* (Fall), 77pp.

Komarovsky, Mirra. Female freshmen view their future: Career salience and its correlates. *Sex Roles,* 1982, *8* (March), 299-314.

Kundsin, Ruth B. (Ed.), *Women and success: The anatomy of achievement.* New York: William Morrow and Co., Inc., 1974.

Kutner, N.G. & Brogan, D.R. The decision to enter medicine: motivations, social support, and discouragements for women. *Psychology of Women Quarterly,* 1980, *5,* 341-57.

Lemert, Edwin M. *Human deviance, social problems and social control,* (2nd Ed.) Englewood Cliffs, N.J.: Prentice-Hall, Inc., 1972.

Lemkau, Jeanne Parr. Personality and Background characteristics of women in male-dominated occupations: A review. *Psychology of Women Quarterly,* Winter 1979, Vol 4(2), 221-40.

Lentz, Linda P. Predicting the career involvement of women one year after college graduation. Paper read at American Educational Research Assn., NY City, March 1982,17pp.

Lentz, Linda P. College selectivity, not college type, is related to graduate women's career aspirations. Paper read at American Educational Research Assn. N Y City, March 1982, 15pp.

Levitin, Teresa E., Quinn, Robert P., & Staines, Graham, L. A woman is 58% of a man. In D.G. McGuigan (Ed.), *New research on women at the University of Michigan,* 1974, pp. 152-57.

Lloyd, Cynthia B. (Ed.), *Sex, discrimination and the division of labor.* New York: Columbia University Press, 1975.

Lloyd, Cynthia B. The division of labor between the sexes: A review. In C.B. Lloyd (Ed.), *Sex, discrimination and the division of labor,,* 1975, 1-24.

Lovett, Sarah L. Personality characteristics and antecedent of vocational choice of graduate women students in science research. *Dissertation Abstracts,* 1969, *29* (12-A), 4287-88.

Lozoff, Marjorie. Fathers and autonomy in women. In R.B. Kundsin (Ed.), *Women and success,* 1974, 103-9.

Lunneborg, Patricia W. Role model influencers of nontraditional professional women. *Journal of Vocational Behavior,* 1982, *20* (June), 276-81.

Lyson, T.A. & Brown, S.S. Sex-role attitudes, curriculum choice, and career ambition: A comparison between women in typical and atypical college majors. *Journal of Vocational Behavior,* 1982, *20* (June), 366-75.

Maccoby, Eleanor. Psychology of sex differences (Lecture), April 1975, University of Cincinnati.

Manis, Jean Denby & Hoffman, Lois Wladis. Fertility motivations and career conflicts in educated women. In D.G. McGuigan (Ed.), *New Research on Women at the University of Michigan,* 1974, pp. 128-30.

Martin, Jane Roland. Excluding women from the educational realm. *Harvard Educational Review,* 1982, *52* (May), 133-48.

Mednick, M.T., Tangri, S.S., & Hoffman, L.W. *Women and achievement-social and motivational analyses.* New York: John Wiley & Sons, 1975.

Merton, Robert K. *Social theory and social structure.* London: The Free Press of Glencoe, Collier-MacMillan, 1964.

Montanelli, J.R., & Mamrak, S. The status of women and minorities in academic computer science. *Communications of the Association for Computing Machinery.* 1976 Oct., *19, #*10, 578-81.

Nagley, D. Traditional and pioneer working mothers. *Journal of Vocational Behavior,* 1971, *T,* 331-41.

Needels-Richardson, Terri L. Factors influencing women's innovative career choices. Poster presentation at the Western Psychological Assn, San Francisco, April 28, 1983, 10pp.

Newsweek. *Women at Work.* December 6,, 1976, pp. 68-81.

O'Connell, Agnes N. Correlates of lifestyle: Personality, role concept, attitudes, influences and choices, *Human Relations* 1980 Aug, *Vol 33* (8), 589-601.

Olesen, Virginia L. & Whittaker, Elvi W. *The silent dialogue, A study in the social psychology of professional socialization.* San Francisco: Jossey-Bass Inc., 1968.

Oritz, Flora Ida. Women and medicine: The process of professional incorporation. *Journal of the American Medical Women's Association,* 1975, Jan., *30,* 18-30.

Orlofsky, Jacob L. & Stake, Jayne E. Psychological masculinity and femininity: relationship to striking and self-concept in the achievement and interpersonal domains. *Psychology of Women Quarterly,* Winter 1981, *Vol 6* (2), 218-33.

Osipow, Samuel H. (Ed.), *Emerging woman: Career analysis and outlooks.* Columbus: A Merrill Professional Textbook in Career Programs Education, A Bell and Howell Co., 1975.

Osipow, Samuel H. Concepts in considering women's careers. In S. Osipow (Ed.), *Emerging woman,* 1975, pp. 1-9.

Parsons, Talcott & Bales, Robert F. *Family, socialization and interaction process.* Glencoe, Illinois: The Free Press, 1955.

Phelps, Stanlee & Austin, Nancy. *The assertive woman.* Virginia: Impact, 1975.

Plas, Jeanne M. & Wallston, Barbara Strudler. Women oriented toward male dominated careers: Is the reference group male or female? *Journal of Counseling Psychology,* 1983, *Vol 30,* No. 1, 46-54.

Rand, Lorraine. Masculinity or femininity? Differentiating career-oriented and homemaking-oriented college freshman woman, 1968. In A. Theodore (Ed.), *The professional woman,* 1971, pp. 156-65.

Randour, M.L., Strasburg, G.L., & Lipmen-Blumen, J. Women in higher education: Trends in enrollments and degrees earned. *Harvard Educational Review,* 1982, *52* (May), 189-202.

Riger, Stephanie. The effects of participation in women's consciousness-raising groups, report of research in progress. In D.G. McGuigan (Ed.), *New Research on Women at the University of Michigan,* 1974, pp. 113-15.

Robinowitz, C.B., Nadelson, C.C. & Notman, M.T. Women in academic psychiatry: Politics and progress. *American Journal of Psychiatry,* 1981, *138* (Oct), 1357-61.

Rosenberg, B.G. & Sutton-Smith, B. Family interaction effects on masculinity-femininity. *Journal of Personality and Social Psychology,* 1968, *8,* 117-20.

Rossi, Alice S. Barriers to the career choice of engineering, medicine, or science among American women. In J.A. Mattfeld & C.G. Van Aken (Eds.), *Women and the scientific professions,* 1975a, 51-127.

Rossi, Alice S. Women in science: Why so few? 1965c. In A. Theodore (Ed.), *The professional woman,* 1971, 612-28.

Rotter, Julian B., Chance, June E., & Phares, E. Jerry. An introduction to social learning theory. In H. Mischel & W. Mischel (Eds.), *Readings in personality,* 1973, pp. 148-51.

Ruddick, S., & Daniels, P. (Eds.), *Working it out: 23 women writers, artists, scientists and scholars talk about their lives and work.* New York: Pantheon Books, 1977.

Rump, E.E. & Delin, P.S. Differential accuracy in the status-height Phenomenon and an experimental effect. *Journal of Personality and Social Psychology,* 1973, *28,* 343-47.

Safilios-Rothschild, C. *Women and social policy.* Englewood Cliffs, N.J.: Prentice-Hall, Inc., 1974.

Safilios-Rothschild, C. Sex role socialization and sex discrimination: A synthesis and critique of the literature. Wash DC: US Dept of Health, Education and Welfare, 1979.

Saslaw, Rita S. A new student for the eighties: The mature woman. *Educational Horizons,* 1981, *60* (Winter), 41-46.

Schiffler, Richard L. Demographic and social factors in women's work lives. In S. Osipow (Ed.), *Emerging women,* 1975, 10-22.

Scopino, John A. Employment attributes of recent science and engineering graduates. NSF Special Report No. 80-325, National Science Foundation, Oct 1980, 19pp.

Sekaran, Uma. An investigation of the career salience of men and women in dual-career families. *Journal of Vocational Behavior,* 1982, *No. 20,* 111-19.

Siegel, Alberta E. & Curtis, Elizabeth Ann. Familial correlates of orientation toward future employment among college women. *Journal of Educational Psychology,* 1963, *54* (1), 33-37.

Spence, Donald. Career set: A resource through transitions and crises. *International Journal of Aging and Human Development,* 1978-79, *Vol 9* (1), 51-65.

Stafford, R.L. An analysis of consciously recalled motivating factors and subsequent professional involvement for American women in New York State. Unpublished E.Ed. Thesis in School of Education, New York University, 1966.

Stake, Jayne E. & Levitz, Ellen. Career goals of college women and men and perceived achievement-related encouragement, *Psychology of Women Quarterly,* Winter 1979, *Vol 4* (2), 151-59.

Stake, Jayne E. The educator's role in fostering female career aspirations. *Journal of the National Association for Women Deans, Administrators and Counselors,* 1981, *45* (Fall), 3-10.

Steinberg, J.A. The perceptions of professional women as deviants. Unpublished Generals paper in the clinical psychology department, Ohio State University, Columbus, 1976.

Stoloff, C. Who joins women's liberation? *Psychiatry,* 1973, *36,* 325-40.

Super, D. A life-span, life-space approach to career development. *Journal of Vocational Behavior,* 1980, *16,* 282-98.

Sutter, Larry E. & Miller, Herman P. Income differences between men and career women. In J. Huber (Ed.), *Changing women in a changing society,* 1973, 200-212.

Sutton-Smith, Brian & Rosenberg, B.G. *The sibling.* New York, Chicago: Holt, Rinehart & Winston, Inc., 1970.

Tangri, Sandra Schwartz. Determinants of occupational role innovation among college women. *Journal of Social Issues,* 1972, *28,* #2, 177-201.

Tapper, Nancy. Women and higher education in the United States. *Higher Education in Europe,* 1981, *6* (July-Sept), 5-13.

Theodore, Athena (Ed.), *The professional woman.* Cambridge, Mass.: Schenkman Publishing Co., Inc., 1971.

Theodore, Athena. The professional woman: Trends and prospects. In A. Theodore (Ed.), *The professional woman,* 1971, pp. 1-35.

Tucker, L.R. Relations of factor score estimates to their use. *Psychometrika,* 1971, *36,* #4, 427-36.

U.S. Department of Labor. 1979 employment and training report of the President. Wash, DC: US Dept of Labor, 1979.

U.S. Women's Bureau. Twenty facts on women workers. Wash DC: US Department of Labor, August 1979.

Van Meter, Mary Jane S. & Agronow, Samuel J. The stress of multiple roles: The case for role strain among married college women. *Family Relations,* Jan 1982, *Vol 31,* 131-38.

Walker, Alice A. Influence of female role models on career-related attitudes. Paper read at Eastern Psychological Assn, NY City, April 1981, 18pp.

Wallis, L.A., Gilder, H. & Thaler H. Advancement of men and women in medical academia: A pilot study. *JAMA,* 1981, *246* (Nov 20), 2350-53.

White, Martha S. Psychological and social barriers to women in science. *Science,* Oct. 23, 1970, *170,* 413-16.

Williams, Juanita H. (Ed.), *Interpretations of women: Readings in psychology.* Ann Arbor, Mich.: Xerox College Publishing, University Microfilms, A Xerox Education Company, 1973.

Williams, Juanita H. Femininity: A deviancy model of normal personality. In J. Williams (Ed.), *Interpretations of women,* 1973, pp. 289-301.

Wolman, Carol & Frank, Hal. The sexes: Women in business: Bitch, neurotic or poor-little-me. *Psychology Today,* February, 1973, 10.

Wolman, Carol & Frank, Hal. Solo woman in a professional peer group. *American Journal of Orthopsychiatry,* 1975, *45,* #1, 164-71.

Yogev, Sara. Judging the professional woman: Changing research, changing values. *Psychology of Women Quarterly,* Spring 1983, *Vol 7* (3), 219-34.

Yogev, Sara. Do professional women have egalitarian marital relationships? *Journal of Marriage and the Family,* 1981, *43* (Nov), 865-71.

Young, Carlotta Joyner, MacKenzie, Doris Layton & Sherif, Carolyn Wood. In search of token women in academia. *Psychology of Women Quarterly,* Summer 1980, Vol 4(4), 508-25.

Zuckerman, D.M. *Challenging the traditional female role: An exploration of women's attitudes and career aspirations.* The Ohio State University, Columbus, 1977. ERIC ED 134787.

Zuckerman, D.M. Self-concept, family background, and personal traits which predict the life goals and sex-role attitudes of technical college and university women. Unpublished dissertation at The Ohio State University, Columbus, 1977.

Zuckerman, Diana M. Family background, sex-role attitudes, and life goals of technical college and university students. *Sex Roles,* 1981, *7* (Nov), 1109-26.

Zuckerman, Diana M. Pre-medical women at selective liberal arts colleges: self-esteem, self-concept, values and stress. Paper read at American Educational Research Assoc, NY City, March 1982, 8pp.

Zytowski, Donald G. Toward a theory of career development for women. *Personnel and Guidance Journal,* 1969, *47* (7), 660-64.

Index

DATE DUE